DATE DUE

SENSORY CHANGES IN THE ELDERLY

SENSORY CHANGES IN THE ELDERLY

By

Francis B. Colavita, Ph.D.

Associate Professor
Department of Psychology
University of Pittsburgh

CHARLES C THOMAS • PUBLISHER
Springfield • Illinois • U.S.A.

Published and Distributed Throughout the World by

CHARLES C THOMAS ● PUBLISHER

Bannerstone House

301-327 East Lawrence Avenue, Springfield, Illinois, U.S.A.

© *1978, by* CHARLES C THOMAS ● PUBLISHER

ISBN 0-398-03829-5

Library of Congress Catalog Card Number: 78-17793

With **THOMAS BOOKS** *careful attention is given to all details of manufacturing and design. It is the Publisher's desire to present books that are satisfactory as to their physical qualities and artistic possibilities and appropriate for their particular use.* THOMAS BOOKS *will be true to those laws of quality that assure a good name and good will.*

Printed in the United States of America
V-R-2

Library of Congress Cataloging in Publication Data

Colavita, Francis B
    Sensory changes in the elderly.

    Includes index.
    1. Sense-organs--Aging. 2. Senses and sensation.
3. Perception, Disorders of. I. Title.
QP435.C64   612.8   78-17793
ISBN 0-398-03829-5

PREFACE

IT IS difficult for me to think of some people as old, even though they may have lived for seventy or seventy-five years. They are so alert, intelligent, active, and involved in life that I think of them simply as exceptional people rather than exceptional old people. Are these individuals just lucky that some unavoidable biological process has not yet caught up with them? Or is it more than luck? Do we have more control than we realize over whether we will be perceived as "old" people or as people who happen to have lived for a long time? This book represents the current status of my search for the answer to such a question.

Our senses are the means by which we stay in contact with our environment. If our sensory systems are inexorably programmed to fail after sixty-five or seventy years of use, then we will necessarily begin to lose contact with our environment. If, on the other hand, our senses are not so programmed, why do age-related sensory changes occur, and why is withdrawal and lack of involvement so characteristic of the aged?

This is the issue that is treated in the following chapters. It is of such importance that I have tried to present the material in a manner that should be of value to the intelligent layman, not just to someone with a background in sensory processes. I am grateful to the publisher for providing me with a means to share this information.

F.B.C.

CONTENTS

SENSORY CHANGES
IN THE ELDERLY

Chapter 1

DEFINING THE PROBLEM

AT THE present time there are more books, magazine articles, and scientific journals dealing with the aging process and problems of the elderly than ever before. This increased interest in the aging process is due to the fact that the elderly now make up a greater percentage of the population of the United States than at any time in our history. Legislators and government agencies, perhaps in response to the increased "power at the polls" of the elderly, have become increasingly receptive to the idea of appropriating more funds for research into various aspects of the aging process. Whatever their motivation, research that can help us understand the mechanisms of normal aging is certainly a worthwhile undertaking.

In 1900, people aged sixty-five and older made up 4 percent of the population of the United States. It is estimated that by the year 2000 this figure will have risen to well over 10 percent. This makes the elderly the fastest growing minority group in the country. The only requirement for membership in this group is that you have patience and wait your turn. The increase in the absolute number of aged people in the population is due to such factors as better health care, better working conditions and job safety, and better nutrition. The increased proportion of elderly in the population is due to a tendency for families to have fewer children than in previous decades as a result of changing life-styles (more women seeking careers outside the home) and improved methods of birth control. Thus at the present time we have a simultaneous increase in the number of older people and a decrease in the number of children.

There are many aspects of the aging process that are interesting, important, and deserving of attention. Some current topics of interest include sexuality in the elderly, personality changes in old age, economic problems in retirement, attitudes of society toward the elderly, mental illness in the elderly, and so on. Yet in the face of all of these highly interesting topics, I have chosen to limit the scope of this book to sensory changes in the elderly. Some people may perceive this as a rather unfortunate choice. The senses may seem to be a rather dull subject when compared to such high interest topics as sex, personality, money, and mental illness. However, it is my contention that a knowledge of how our senses operate is not only important for understanding the behavior of the elderly, but that such knowledge is also important for understanding all behavior.

Our behavior does not occur spontaneously or haphazardly. Rather, behavior occurs in response to some event that has taken place in our environment. To fully understand behavior, one must understand the way in which environmental events are detected by living creatures. Such an understanding involves at least a basic knowledge of how the various sensory systems function.

The way that we perceive the world around us is determined by the characteristics of our sensory systems. Different animals (including human beings, as we shall see) may live in the same physical environment but have entirely different perceptions of this physical environment because their sensory systems have different ranges of sensitivity. We can refer to the way that an organism perceives its physical environment as that organism's *perceptual world.*

Some examples of how the characteristics of different animals' sensory systems directly influence their perceptual worlds may be of value here. Many people have cats as household pets. Since the cat is living in the same physical environment as we are, it might be assumed that the cat's perceptual world is the same as ours. This assumption would be totally false. In some ways the cat's perceptual world is much richer than ours, and in other ways its perceptual world is impoverished compared to ours. Take the case of color vision. Unless we are colorblind, the human eye is sensitive to a wide range of hues and colors. This portion of our perceptual world is unavailable to the cat. The receptors in the cat's visual system are not sensitive to different colors. Whereas human beings have no trouble obeying traffic lights on the basis of color, the cat would have to obey the lights on the basis of position.

On the other hand, the cat's auditory system is sensitive to sounds with pitches over three times higher than the most sensitive human ear can detect, so the cat's auditory perceptual world is much broader than ours. Often the cat can be seen to prick up its ears and appear to be attending to something, but we can detect no sound at all. The cat's sense of smell is also much more acute than that of the human being. A mother cat can identify her kittens on the basis of their smell, and kittens can identify their mother on the basis of her smell, even before they are old enough for their eyes to have opened. Thus the olfactory perceptual world of the cat is much richer than that of its owner. We have a situation where the cat wonders why we step on the brake pedal of the car, because its perceptual world does not contain the red color of the stoplight. We, in turn, wonder why the cat suddenly pricks up its ears, because our perceptual world does not include certain high-pitched sounds made by rodents. We are surprised that a kitten with its eyes as yet unopened begins crying when its mother moves soundlessly away from it, because the odor of the mother cat is not a part of our perceptual world.

The above examples should suffice to show that an animal's behavior is not determined directly by its physical environment, but rather by that part of the physical environment that its sensory receptors can detect, its perceptual world. Because the receptors of different animals have different sensitivity charac-teristics, different animals live in different perceptual worlds. Just as different species such as cats and humans live in dif-ferent perceptual worlds, so can different individuals of the same species live in different perceptual worlds. As an extreme example of this, deaf persons, blind persons, or anosmic (lacking the sense of smell) persons all live in perceptual worlds that are different from each other and different from the perceptual world of someone who has the use of all of those senses.

The chapters to follow will be concerned with the sensory abilities of human beings, and how these abilities change in old age. It is true in general that our sensory systems become less acute with age. This implies that the perceptual world of the elderly differs in predictable ways from the perceptual world of the child or the young adult. Some of these perceptual differences will be described in the pages to follow.

The idea that the sensitivity of our eyes and our ears is going to decline as we grow older is greeted with fear by some and with shame by others. Neither of these reactions is appropriate, in that they only make an inevitable situation that much worse. The most appropriate reaction to the decline in sensory abilities which occurs with age is to become informed as to what changes to expect, to compensate for these changes when possible, and to learn to make greater use of our remaining sensory capacities.

It is generally the case that an understanding of some undesirable but unavoidable situation permits people to deal with the situation more intelligently and with less anxiety. My hope is that the information contained in the following pages will help provide an understanding of the changes that are known to occur in human sensory systems as a function of the aging process.

The general plan of the following chapters is to begin by providing some background information about how each sensory system operates at its peak level of performance. Then those physical changes likely to occur as a consequence of the aging process will be indicated. Next, a description will be given of how these physical changes can bring about an alteration of the individual's perceptual world. Finally, some suggestions will be made for keeping age-related sensory changes to a minimum.

Chapter 2

THE VISUAL SYSTEM

Background

WHILE it is not necessarily true for all animals, in the case of human beings it is clear that vision is our most important and relied-upon sense. In order to see we need light; what we refer to as light is actually electromagnetic energy. Electromagnetic energy travels outward from its source (the sun, a reading lamp, etc.) in waves, much like the ripples in a pond travel outward from the spot in the water where a stone has been thrown. However, while the ripples in a pond may travel at a speed of only a few inches per second, light waves travel at the incredible speed of *186,000 miles per second.* Still using our analogy of ripples in a pond to help describe the characteristics of light, the term *wavelength* refers to the distance between the crest of each successive ripple. The wavelength of the ripples produced by throwing a small stone into a pond might be only a few inches, while the wavelength of large waves in the ocean might be many feet. In contrast to this relatively small range, the spectrum of electromagnetic energy extends from the x rays, with a wavelength of one nanometer (a nanometer is one billionth of a meter), up to radio broadcast waves with a wavelength of 100 meters. The range of electromagnetic energy is depicted in Figure 1. Not all of this total electromagnetic spectrum is perceived by us as light. Rather, the visible spectrum is made up of a very small region ranging from 400 nanometers to 700 nanometers.

As indicated in Figure 1, the color of light is determined by the wavelength of electromagnetic energy. A wavelength of 700 nanometers is perceived as red light, while wavelengths of around 400 nanometers are seen as violet. White light is made up of a mixture of all the wavelengths of the visible spectrum.

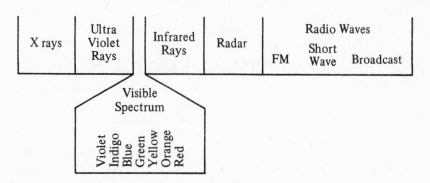

Figure 1. The electromagnetic energy spectrum. The human eye is sensitive only to a small segment of the spectrum located between the ultraviolet and infrared rays.

This can be demonstrated by shining a white light source (such as sunlight) through a prism, and observing what appears on a viewing surface such as a wall. It can be shown that white light breaks down into the colors red, orange, yellow, green, blue, indigo, and violet. Figure 2 diagrams the breakdown of white light into its component parts. A memory aid to help recall the order of the colors in the visible spectrum is to remember the name ROY G. BIV. Each letter in this ficticious name stands for one of the colors in its proper order. The next time you have the opportunity to observe the colors of a rainbow, which is formed when sunlight shines through moisture droplets left in the air after it has rained, you will see that here again the order ROYGBIV is maintained. The moisture droplets are essentially acting as a prism, breaking the sunlight down into its component colors.

The reason for this characteristic ordering of the colors of the visible spectrum is because different wavelengths of light have different indices of *refraction*. Refraction refers to the tendency of light rays to be deflected from a straight line of travel as they pass from a less dense medium (air) through a more dense medium (the glass of the prism). The short wavelengths of light are deflected more than the longer wavelengths, and as a consequence the wavelengths that make up white light are

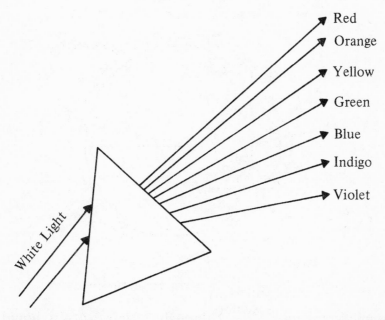

Figure 2. White light is broken down into its component colors when passed through a prism. The short wavelengths are bent more than the long wavelengths, resulting in an orderly arrangement from red through violet.

segregated into their component colors, ordered from the long (red) wavelengths to the short (violet) wavelengths, when passed through a prism.

The human brain, which is the ultimate source of our perception, is not directly sensitive to electromagnetic energy (light). Only the visual receptors in our eyes are sensitive to light. It is the job of our visual receptors to act as transducers, being stimulated by light waves and in turn generating weak electrical impulses which travel to the brain by way of the optic nerve. The electrical impulses which travel to our brain by way of the optic nerve are interpreted by the brain as visual sensations.

Let us now examine some of the processes that must take place in the eye in order for us to perceive light. The anatomy of the human eye is depicted in Figure 3. Light enters the eye

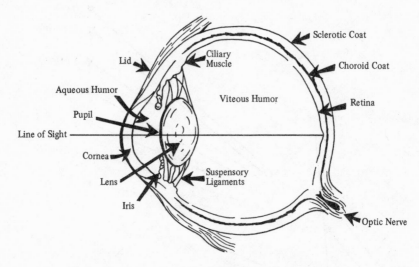

Figure 3. Anatomy of the human eye in cross section.

through the *cornea*, passes through a clear, viscous liquid known as the *aqueous humor,* then passes through an opening in the *iris* known as the *pupil.* The light next travels through the *lens* and the *vitreous humor* fluid before arriving at the retina at the back of the eyeball. The retina contains the visual receptors which convert light into electrical impulses. These electrical impulses then leave the eye by way of the *optic nerve* and travel to the visual portions of the brain.

A more detailed view of the retina is presented in Figure 4. As shown in this figure, the retina is actually composed of three distinct layers: the receptor layer, the bipolar cell layer, and the ganglion cell layer. There are two kinds of receptor cells in the human retina, named *rods* and *cones* because of their characteristic shapes. Cones are responsible for our color vision and require bright light for adequate functioning. Rods are responsible for vision under conditions of dim lighting and are unable to distinguish different colors.

Light entering the eye produces a bleaching effect in light-sensitive chemicals (called photopigments) contained in the rods and cones. The bipolar and ganglion cells then convert

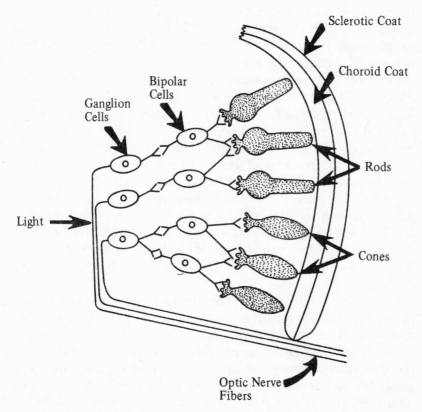

Figure 4. Schematic representation of the three layers of the retina. Light must pass through the ganglion cell and bipolar cell layers before reaching the rods and cones.

this chemical disturbance in the receptors into electrical impulses for transmission to the brain. Human beings possess what is referred to as an inverted retina, in that (Figure 4) light entering the eye must pass through the ganglion cell and bipolar cell layers before it reaches the light-sensitive rods and cones. One would think that perhaps a more efficient way to design an eye would be to have the rods and cones in front of the bipolar and ganglion cell layers. However, the problem with having the rods and cones in front of the bipolar and ganglion cells is that rods and cones need a rich blood supply to maintain their normal metabolic activity, and the major blood supply in the eyeball is behind the retina. If the blood supply were in front of the retina, it would interfere with the passage of light to the receptors.

Each of our eyes contains approximately 120 million rods and 6.5 million cones. These receptors are not evenly distributed over the retina. Rather, a small central region of the retina called the *fovea* is densely populated with cones but contains no rods. As one moves from the fovea toward the periphery of the retina, the number of cones decreases and the number of rods increases. The fovea is that portion of the retina that we use when we read a book or do any other task requiring fine discrimination in adequate lighting. You would not think of trying to read a book by looking at it out of the corner of your eye; this would focus the image of the book on the rods, which do not have good resolving power and are better suited for night vision.

As was mentioned earlier, visual sensations depend upon the presence of light-sensitive photopigments in the rods and cones. In the presence of light, these photopigments are bleached and actually change their chemical composition. In the human retina, one rod pigment (rhodopsin) and three cone pigments (erythrolabe, chlorolabe, and cyanolabe) have been identified. It is the cone pigments that are sensitive to different colors. Erythrolabe (the red catcher) is sensitive to red light, chlorolabe (the green catcher) is sensitive to green light, and cyanolabe (the blue catcher) is sensitive to blue light. Our ability to see different colors is determined by the amount of bleaching in each of these three types of cone pigments that a visual stimulus produces. All colors that can be seen by the normal human eye can be produced by the proper mixture of red, green, and blue.

The phenomenon of colorblindness occurs when a person has a reduced level of (or is entirely lacking) one or more of the cone pigments. A person can be red blind, green blind, or more rarely, blue blind depending upon which cone pigment is affected. Colorblindness is known to be a hereditary condition. Men are usually the victims of colorblindness, while women are usually the carriers of the condition. It is estimated that around 5 percent of the male population has some degree of color-blindness or color weakness, while only 0.1 percent of the female population is colorblind.

With this simple overview of how electromagnetic energy from the environment is translated into the perception of light, let us move on to our primary interest, which is how the visual system is affected by the aging process. Perhaps the easiest way to accomplish this purpose is to take each of the parts of the eye labeled in Figure 3, briefly describe the function of each part, indicate what if any physical change occurs with age, and relate this physical change to alterations in visual ability.

Physical Changes

The Sclerotic Coat

The sclerotic coat is the tough, fibrous outermost layer of the eyeball. While the sclerotic coat does not contribute directly to our visual ability, it does serve a protective function and is the point of attachment for the muscles that move the eyeball. The sclerotic coat is the well known "whites of the eyes" that the colonial minutemen were supposed to see in the redcoats before they fired their rifles. In older people the sclerotic coat appears to contain more lipids (fats) than in younger individuals. The functional significance of this change in fat content is not known.

THE CORNEA: The cornea is actually a frontal extension of the sclerotic coat. The cornea, although it appears to be transparent, actually acts as a protective filter and keeps light in the ultraviolet range from entering the eye. Light in this range (approximately 380 nanometers) could do harm to the sensitive receptors on the retina if it were permitted to reach them. In addition to guarding the retina from ultraviolet light, the cornea also acts as an optical instrument, working in conjunction with the lens of the eye to bring images into sharp focus on the retina.

One characteristic sign of aging in humans that involves the cornea is the formation of the *arcus senilis,* or senile ring. This refers to an opaque ring just inside the border between the cornea and the sclerotic coat. In most individuals, some evidence of formation of the arcus senilis is present by age fifty, although the completed ring may not be apparent until some time in the sixties. One obvious consequence of the arcus senilis is a reduction in peripheral vision, because only diffuse light can pass through the opaque ring. This brings about a slight shrinking of the visual field.

Occasionally, injury, infection, or wartlike growths will cloud large regions of the cornea and produce a severe inability to see shapes and forms. In such a case, physicians may resort to a corneal transplant in an attempt to restore useful vision to the afflicted individual. The corneal tissue that is used in these transplants comes from people who have designated that their eyes be used for this purpose after death. Corneal transplants appear to be remarkably free from the tissue rejection problems that are encountered in heart and kidney transplant procedures. This may be due to the cornea's lack of a significant blood supply.

The Iris and the Pupil

For reasons that will soon become obvious, these two parts of the eye can be considered together. The iris is the circular structure located behind the cornea. The iris contains different colored pigments in different individuals, so that the iris' color (commonly refered to as eye color) may range from light blue to black. The color of the iris is one of the physical traits in human beings that is known to have a hereditary basis. Thus, blue eyes tend to run in some families, and brown eyes in other families. If a blue eyed individual and a brown eyed individual have children, the offspring are more likely to inherit brown iris color. For this reason, brown eye (iris) color is what the geneticists refer to as a dominant characteristic, while blue eye (iris) color is called a recessive characteristic.

The pupil is not actually a structure; rather, it is a hole in the center of the iris. An ophthalmologist can actually look through the pupil and see the retina. The diameter of the pupil changes reflexively as a function of light intensity. In bright light, a sphincter muscle contracts the iris, causing the pupil to become smaller. This cuts down on the amount of light entering the eye and protects sensitive retinal elements from over-stimulation. In dim light the iris dilates, making the pupil larger and allowing more light to enter the eye. This dilation maximizes the probability of detecting a visual stimulus in dim light. The pupil can change its diameter over a surprisingly wide range, from less than 2 millimeters in bright light to more than 8 millimeters in the very dim light.

Interestingly, another aspect of a visual stimulus (in addition to brightness) has been shown to affect pupil size. Doctor Eck-hard Hess of the University of Chicago has reported that how one feels emotionally about the object that is being viewed can affect the size of the pupil, independent of light intensity. Doctor Hess's studies show that when looking at something we like, the pupil actually increases its diameter, while constriction occurs when we look at something that we do not like. Thus, under the same level of illumination, the pupils will increase in size when we view a loved one but decrease in size when viewing a snake (unless the viewer happens to be fond of snakes). As an interesting aside, Doctor Hess also reported the somewhat sexist finding that women with large pupils are found more attractive by men than are women with small pupils.

A number of changes are known to occur in the iris and pupil as a function of advancing age. Perhaps the most obvious change is a gradual fading of the color in the iris. This fading, especially noticeable in people with light-colored eyes, is due to a tendency in older people for the pigment granules which give the iris its color to change their location and move toward the periphery of the iris. This migration of color pigments causes maximal fading around the border of the pupil. There is a potentially dangerous aspect to this change in pigment distribution within the iris. It is possible for small amounts of pigment granule, along with minute portions of the material that forms the lens, to be carried away by the aqueous humor fluid located between the lens and the cornea (see Fig. 3) and help set up obstructions that lead to *glaucoma.* The aqueous humor fluid is constantly being produced, and in the normal eye it is free to circulate through a series of passageways. When these passageways become obstructed, possibly by the collection of pigment granules from the iris or by small particles that have been sloughed off of the lens, accumulation of the aqueous humor fluid causes a buildup of pressure in the eyeball. In severe cases, this pressure buildup can cause retinal damage and lead to blindness.

Another serious change in the iris known to occur with age is a tendency for the tissue around the border of the pupil to swell. This swelling interferes with the ability of the pupil to dilate in response to decreased levels of illumination, and in extreme cases dilation is completely eliminated. This produces a reduction in pupil size and is a factor in the reduced visual sensitivity generally reported in older people, since reduced amounts of light are now entering the eye. Reduction in visual acuity in the elderly is especially prominent in dim light.

The Lens

The lens of the eye, located immediately behind the iris, is actually an optical instrument that can change its shape. The cornea and lens together form the optical system of the eye, bringing the image of objects in the visual field into sharp focus on the retina. The lens is made up of layers of transparent-appearing membranes, assembled in the manner of an onion. The lens is referred to as a variable optical instrument in that it can change its focal length by altering its curvature. This ability of the lens to change its curvature in order to bring objects at varying distances into focus is referred to as *accommodation.* The mechanism that produces accommodation of the lens involves contraction of the ciliary muscle (see Fig. 3, which releases tension on the *suspensory ligaments.* The lens, having elastic properties, automatically bulges out when tension is reduced on the suspensory ligaments. Thus, for viewing objects that are close to us (near vision), the ciliary

muscle contracts, tension is reduced on the suspensory ligaments, the lens bulges (becomes shorter and fatter), and the
near object is brought to focus on the retina. When viewing
objects at a distance, the ciliary muscle is relaxed, tension is
maintained on the suspensory ligaments, and the lens is pulled
into a more elongated and flat shape. This configuration of the
lens brings far objects into focus on the retina. Continuous use
of the eyes in tasks requiring near vision, such as sewing or
reading, can produce what is generally called "eye strain" due
to prolonged contraction of the ciliary muscle. It is actually the
ciliary muscle, not the visual receptors, that become fatigued
when we experience eye strain. It has been suggested in this
regard that individuals who are engaged in prolonged
near work can relieve some of the strain by periodically looking
into the distance and temporarily relaxing the ciliary muscle.

Several changes in the lens are known to be associated with
the aging process. Perhaps the most widely known change is
the loss of elasticity, which interferes with the process of accommodation. A loss of the lens's elastic properties reduces its
ability to bulge out and increase its curvature when the ciliary
muscle contracts. This leads to the condition known as *presbyopia*, a decreased ability to focus on near objects. Investigation
of the ciliary muscle in human cadavers has suggested that in
elderly people there is a tendency for lipid (fat) accumulations
to occur. Thus it is possible that, in addition to loss of elasticity
in the lens, further deficits in accommodation may occur due to
these layers of fat interfering with the ability of the ciliary
muscle to contract to the same degree that was possible at an
earlier age.

Another condition seen to occur in the aging lens is the
development of cataracts. By the time a person reaches seventy
years of age, some evidence of cataract formation is the rule, not
the exception. Cataract involves an opacification (loss of transparency) in the lens of the eye. The term nuclear cataract is
applied when the center of the lens is affected, while the term
cortical cataract denotes a condition where the surface layers of
the lens become clouded. One obvious consequence of cataracts

is interference with visual acuity. This interference may reach such an extreme that the individual may lose all patterned vision, being able to detect only shades of lightness and darkness.

One final age-related change in the lens should be mentioned. There is a tendency for the tissue of the lens to lose its transparency and take on a yellowish color. As a consequence, the lens begins to filter out certain wavelengths of light, which results in an impairment in color vision with age. Color sensitivity in the elderly has been shown to fall off across the entire visible spectrum. However, it is especially noticeable for the short wavelengths at the blue-violet end of the spectrum while being less serious at long wavelengths, the red end of the spectrum. There is an interesting demonstration of this decreased sensitivity of elderly persons to the blue-violet portion of the visible spectrum that we may all have had occasion to observe at one time or another. We sometimes see elderly women who appear to have a bluish coloration in their hair. This is probably a consequence of the fact that these women are not aware of just how blue their hair looks because of their decreased sensitivity to the short wavelength end of the visible spectrum. They use a hair rinse that looks good to them, and they assume that it looks the same to everyone else.

The Retina

We have already mentioned the retina of the eye with its three layers: the receptor layer, the bipolar cell layer, and the ganglion cell layer. With the exception of extreme pathological conditions such as detached retina (to be discussed later), the retina appears to be relatively free from age-related changes. Thus, the reductions in visual acuity and in color discrimination associated with the aging process are more likely due to changes in the eye's optical instruments, the lens and cornea.

The Choroid Coat

The choroid coat is the layer of tissue located between the

retina and the sclerotic coat. In human beings, the choroid coat has two major functions. First, it supplies nutrition to the retina by means of its blood supply. Second, the choroid coat is responsible for absorbing any stray light that might be present in the interior of the eye. If, as sometimes happens, all of the light that enters the eye is not absorbed by photopigment molecules in the rods and cones, this stray light could actually be reflected from the back of the eyeball and stimulate the rods and cones from the wrong direction. Since visual receptors cannot determine which direction the light that stimulates them comes from, stray light bouncing around in the eyeball would produce a blurred image and interfere with our visual acuity. By absorbing stray light, the choroid coat actually increases our visual acuity by permitting the rods and cones to be stimulated only by light entering the eye from the forward direction.

We started this discussion of the choroid coat by saying that "in human beings it has these two functions." We specified "in human beings" because the choroid coat has a different function in certain nonhuman animals. In nocturnal creatures such as the cat and the raccoon, the choroid coat actually reflects stray light rather than absorbing it. Most of us have had the experience of seeing the eyes of a cat or raccoon at night when a flashlight or a car's headlights are shined on the animal. The eyes of the creature shine in the dark like two glowing coals. We are actually observing the light being reflected off the animal's choroid coat. A light shined in a human eye at night would produce no such effect.

The reflecting choroid coat of the nocturnal animal actually increases its visual sensitivity at night. If light entering the eye of a nocturnal creature should not be absorbed by a visual receptor on the way into the eye, the animal gets another chance to detect the light when it is reflected off the choroid coat. This second chance to detect the light is of great importance to nocturnal animals who are active when illumination is very poor. Nocturnal creatures tolerate the blurred image that results from the reflection of stray light from the back of the eye, in return for a second chance to detect an object in very dim light.

While the cat has greater sensitivity than humans have in dim light, the human eye has greater acuity than the cat under normal levels of illumination. Sensitivity and acuity are not the same thing. Sensitivity means that the animal can tell "something is out there," while acuity means "something is out there and I know what it is." The cat has greater sensitivity than man in that it can detect objects in dim light. However, the human eye is more able to identify what the object is once there is enough light for us to see it. It has been estimated that, in daylight, the acuity of the human eye is ten times greater than that of the cat eye.

Some changes in the human choroid coat have been reported to occur as a consequence of advancing age. These changes involve the blood vessels of the choroid coat. Either arteriosclerosis (hardening of the arteries) or atherosclerosis (accumulated cholesterol-lipid material in the blood vessels), or both, may be seen. These vascular changes do not directly affect vision, although they can have indirect consequences because the retina depends upon the vessels of the choroid coat for nutrition. Possibly, impairment of the nutrition of the retina is responsible for the reduced levels of dark adaptation generally found in older persons. As we are all aware, time spent in the dark increases the sensitivity of the visual system. The sensitivity increase comes about because visual photopigments in the rods and cones that are continually being bleached in the light are allowed to regenerate to their full extent in the dark. This increased visual sensitivity as a function of time spent in darkness is known as *dark adaptation*. Its effects are quite noticeable upon walking out of a dark movie theater into the afternoon sunlight. The sunlight seems unbearably bright at first, but after several minutes it does not seem to be nearly as bright. The brightness of the sunlight did not change during those few minutes. Rather, the sensitivity of the visual system changed. When you first walked out into the sunlight the eye was in a dark-adapted state and the visual photopigments in the receptors were at full strength. After several minutes in the light, some bleaching of the photopigments occurred and the sunlight no longer was perceived as being so bright.

Dark adaptation is essentially complete after a person has spent forty minutes in the dark. The rate of dark adaptation does not appear to change in older people; their visual systems still reach the greatest level of sensitivity after forty minutes in the dark. What does appear to change is the final level of sensitivity that is achieved. Older people can no longer achieve the same final level of sensitivity that they could reach when they were younger. This decrease in dark adaptation may be attributable at least in part to vascular changes in the choroid coat.

The Optic Nerve

The optic nerve is composed of many individual nerve fibers originating in the ganglion cell layer of the retina. Electrical activity occurring in bipolar and ganglion cells as a result of light bleaching the photopigments in the receptors is transmitted to the brain by way of the optic nerve at speeds of up to 100 meters per second. It is generally believed that age-related changes in the optic nerve are relatively slight. Except for pathological conditions such as tumors of the optic nerve, reductions in visual ability seen in the elderly do not appear to be based upon altered functioning of the optic nerve.

Suggestions

The physical changes in the eye discussed in the preceeding pages suggest that reductions in visual acuity, presbyopia, reduced color sensitivity, narrowing of the peripheral visual field, and decreased sensitivity in low levels of illumination are fairly common occurrences in older people. Given that such changes are likely to occur, how do we deal with them intelligently? First of all, recognizing that visual abilities in dim light are especially affected, older people can take steps to increase the available lighting. This might involve procedures as simple as replacing existing light bulbs with bulbs of a higher wattage. It would also be advisable for older people who·are accustomed to driving cars or piloting planes to recognize that extra precautions should be exercised at night. Poor night vision can also be the result of a vitamin A deficiency, as vitamin A is an important component of visual photopigments. All people, but especially older people who will experience reduced visual sensitivity from other causes, should be aware that good vision requires proper nutrition. It might also be mentioned that proper nutrition can help minimize the vascular changes such as arteriosclerosis and atherosclerosis sometimes seen in the blood vessels of the choroid coat.

The loss of elasticity of the lens, with the resulting decrease in the ability of this structure to undergo accommodation, can be compensated for by the use of bifocal eye glasses. There should be no embarrassment attached to the wearing of bifocals, although some individuals are reluctant to admit that they require glasses for reading or for close work. A recent informal survey made in an undergraduate psychology class revealed the somewhat interesting finding that older people who wear bifocals are perceived as being intelligent, possibly because they look as though they read a lot.

The more serious physical changes in the eye that can occur with age (cataracts, detached retina, and glaucoma) can also be dealt with, although more extreme procedures are involved. A seriously clouded lens can be surgically removed, and eyeglasses can provide the missing optical properties needed to bring images into sharp focus on the retina. Medical procedures also exist for treating detached retinas. Most cases of detached retina occur when a tear develops in the tissue of the retina and the vitreous humor fluid is allowed to run through the tear and separate the retina from the choroid coat. The treatment for this condition is to locate the tear, create an inflammatory reaction around the tear (a small laser beam has recently been used for this purpose), place the retina against the inflammation, and keep the patient immobile until the inflammation turns into a scar. The scar seals the tear and prevents the vitreous fluid from forcing its way between the retina and the choroid coat.

Glaucoma, a hardening of the eyeball due to buildup of pressure in the aqueous humor fluid, can be treated and controlled by drugs that lower the pressure in the eyeball.

One final word of caution is in order regarding the visual system. It is well known that prolonged exposure to loud noises can have permanent harmful effects on our hearing. Less well known is the fact that prolonged exposure to bright light may similarly have long term desensitizing affects on the visual sensitivity. In one study of visual sensitivity, the eyesight of lifeguards who had spent the entire summer in bright sunlight was found to be somewhat desensitized even several months after the swimming season had ended. Good advice for everyone would be to wear sunglasses when exposed to bright sunlight. In view of the fact that vision is our most important and most frequently relied upon sense, it is deserving of the best attention that we can provide it.

Chapter 3

THE AUDITORY SYSTEM

Background

THE auditory system is our second most important means of perceiving environmental events at a distance from our bodies. The ear permits us to detect and respond to stimuli which are physically distant from us, and even to approximate the location of a sound source. However, we must typically use our eyes to fix the exact location in space of a sound-producing object.

Although we do not usually think of it as such, the auditory system is actually a highly sensitive touch system. When we "hear" something, we are actually responding to a complex pattern of air molecules colliding with and producing small movements of the eardrums. We will explain shortly how vibration of the eardrum (or *tympanic membrane* as it is more formally known) can result in the generation of electrical impulses in the auditory nerve which travel to the brain and create the perception of sound.

Sound is produced when some vibrating object, such as the arms of the tuning fork, a radio speaker, or a set of human vocal cords, transmits its vibratory action to the air molecules surrounding it. The initially disturbed air molecules in turn produce vibratory activity in the air molecules next to them, and eventually the vibrations reach the air molecules next to the eardrum; these air molecules induce the eardrum itself to vibrate.

There are two results from the nature of sound transmission as briefly explained above. First, there can be no sound if there is no medium to conduct vibrations from the sound source to the ear. Thus, there is no sound in a vacuum, because there are no air molecules to transmit vibrations. This fact can be demonstrated in an elementary physics experiment. A wind-up alarm clock is suspended in a bell jar, and then the air is evacuated from the jar. As the air gets thinner, the sound of the alarm grows progressively fainter and when all of the air has been removed from the jar the sound stops, even though one can see that the clapper of the alarm is still striking. Returning the air to the bell jar causes the sound of the alarm to recur. The second point regarding sound transmission is that sound must travel at a measurable speed, and this speed will depend upon the characteristics of the conducting medium. Ordinarily, the medium through which sound waves are transmitted is air, but sound can also travel in gasses other than air, in water, in wood, in steel, and in many other media. For example, one can hear a train approaching in the distance by putting one's ear to the track. In this case the sound vibrations are being transmitted from the train to our eardrum by the steel rail.

In air, the speed of sound is around 1110 feet per second. When one compares this rate of conduction with the speed of light, which is 186,000 miles per second, it is easy to understand why in a storm we see the flash of lightning well before we hear the clap of thunder. The relatively slow speed at which sound travels has now been taken into account in important athletic competitions such as the Olympics. In the swimming and running events, for instance, the traditional starting gun is no longer used. Rather, a beeping sound occurs simultaneously from small speakers located under each starting block. This procedure takes away the slight time advantage that used to go to those athletes in the lanes closest to the starting gun. The sound of the gun would actually reach their ears several thousandths of a second before it would reach the ears of the competitors in the lanes more distant from the gun.

The speed at which sound travels varies with environmental temperature, and also with the density of the conducting medium. Sound travels faster in warm air than in cold air, because at a higher temperature the air molecules are more volatile and it is easier to induce vibrations in them. Regarding the density of the conducting medium, the speed of sound in a railroad track would be around 16,500 feet per second compared to 1110 feet per second in air. The steel of the rail of course has a much greater density than air, and thus conducts sound many times faster than air.

Two important characteristics of a vibrating object are (1) its frequency of vibration and (2) its amplitude of vibration. Frequency refers to how rapidly the vibrations occur over time, and amplitude refers to the distance that the object moves in a single vibration cycle. The frequency with which an object vibrates determines the pitch of the sound that we perceive. The more times per second that the eardrum is made to vibrate, the higher will be the pitch of the perceived sound. The amplitude of the vibration, on the other hand, determines the loudness of the perceived sound. The vibratory frequency of a tone is usually specified in cycles per second, or Hertz (Hz). Hertz is used as the unit of measurement for frequency in tribute to H. R. Hertz, a German physicist who died in 1894. The amplitude or intensity of a tone is usually specified in decibels, abbreviated dB. Zero dB is the loudness at which a normal young listener can just detect a faint sound, while 100 dB is the point where sound becomes so loud that it is perceived as painful. The faint ticking of a watch that can barely be heard when held at arm's length in a quiet room probably has a loudness level of 0 dB, while an enormous thunder clap directly overhead would have a loudness level of around 100 dB. (As a rule of thumb, it is not a good idea to expose one's ears to sounds of 80 dB or more for any appreciable length of time, as such exposure could cause hearing loss.) To give an idea of the extreme sensitivity of the auditory system, the faint ticking of the watch mentioned in the example above need only displace the eardrum a distance of 10^{-9} centimeters (less than the diameter of a hydrogen atom) in a healthy young listener before a sound is perceived.

The main point of the above discussion is that the physical stimulus for hearing is rapid in and out movement of the eardrum, produced (usually) by pressure variations in the air molecules adjacent to the eardrum. The human ear is sensitive to frequencies of vibration ranging approximately from 20 to 20,000 Hz, although this range can vary significantly in different people. In attempting to describe how small rapid vibrations of the eardrum end up producing auditory sensations, frequent reference will be made to the structures of the ear presented in Figures 5, 6, and 7.

As was the case in our treatment of the visual system, we will first describe the workings of the auditory system at its normal level of efficiency, and then indicate how age-related changes in the system may lower this level.

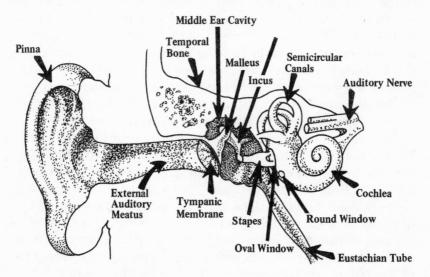

Figure 5. Anatomy of the human ear, depicting the structures comprising the outer ear, middle ear, and inner ear.

Physical Changes

The Outer Ear

This designation includes the *pinna,* the *external auditory meatus* or ear canal, and the *tympanic membrane* or eardrum. As most people are aware, lower animals such as dogs and cats have the ability to move the pinna and turn it toward the source of a sound to enhance detection. Human beings, on the other hand, must resort to the device of cupping a hand to the ear to maximize the collection of sound waves. Actually, the human pinna still contains vestigal muscles for movement, but in most people these muscles are atrophied and not functional. Some individuals can make use of these muscles to wiggle their ears to entertain their friends, but this is about the extent of the human's ability to move the pinna.

THE EXTERNAL AUDITORY MEATUS: The meatus, or ear canal, is the passageway which leads from the outside world to the eardrum. In the adult human, the auditory meatus is approximately 37 millimeters in length. The length of the ear canal actually contributes to the hearing sensitivity of the human ear. When audiologists test the auditory sensitivity of a human patient, they find that the normal ear is not equally sensitive to all frequencies between 20 and 20,000 Hz. Rather, the human ear is relatively insensitive at the upper and lower ends of the audible frequency range, but quite sensitive in the mid range, especially from 1500 to 3000 Hz. This turns out to be a fortunate range, in that many important speech sounds occur in this range. As was alluded to above, the length of the ear canal actually contributes to the sensitivity of the human ear to frequencies around 3000 Hz, because the ear canal is actually a column of air closed at one end by the eardrum; closed columns of air actually amplify different sound frequencies as a function of the length and diameter of the column. Every child learns that one can produce a whistling sound by blowing down the neck of a soda pop bottle, and that the pitch of the sound is higher when the bottle is quite full, with the pitch getting progressively lower as one drinks more of the contents of the bottle. As the bottle is emptied, we are lengthening the column of air in the bottle and lowering its resonance frequency. A very small pop bottle, having the length and diameter of the ear canal, would produce a whistling sound with a pitch of around 3000 Hz if it was blown into. The ear canal is smaller in children than it is in adults, giving it a higher resonance frequency; not surprisingly, audiologists report that children are sensitive to higher tonal frequencies than are adults. In general, the smaller the animal the higher its upper frequency for hearing, because the resonance frequency characteristics of its auditory structures are higher. Thus, dogs and cats can hear frequencies much higher than the human ear can detect.

THE TYMPANIC MEMBRANE: The tympanic membrane, or eardrum, is a thin piece of tissue located at the interior end of the ear canal. Vibration of the air molecules in the ear canal impose vibrations on the eardrum. These vibrations are in turn transmitted to the structures of the middle ear, which will be discussed below. Two characteristics of the eardrum worthy of mention are (1) it is approximately 65 square millimeters in surface area and (2) it is densely populated with pain receptors. A ruptured eardrum is quite painful for this reason.

The Middle Ear

As shown in Figure 5, the middle ear contains three small bones known collectively as the *ossicles*. The middle ear also contains two tiny muscles known as the *stapedius muscle* and the *tensor tympani muscle,* as well as the *eustachian tube*. It is the job of the three ossicles — the malleus, incus, and stapes (sometimes referred to as the hammer, anvil, and stirrup because of their shapes) — to transmit vibrations from the eardrum to the inner ear. In the inner ear these vibrations are converted into electrical impulses which travel to the brain by way of the auditory nerve. The mechanism by which these electrical impulses are generated will be described later. The middle ear muscles serve a protective function. These small muscles are attached to the ossicles such that when the muscles contract, they reduce the ability of the ossicles to transmit vibrations to the inner ear. The protective function comes about because the stapedius and tensor tympani contract reflexly to loud noises, interfering with the movement of the ossicles, and helping to prevent damage to the sensitive structures of the inner ear. Some individuals have the ability to voluntarily contract their stapedius and tensor tympani muscles. Occasionally, these muscles contract when we swallow or yawn, producing a brief crackling sound that we can actually hear if we listen for it.

THE EUSTACHIAN TUBE: This is the passageway leading from

the middle ear to the nasopharynx (back of the throat). The eustachian tube permits us to equalize the air pressure on both sides of the eardrum. Yawning or swallowing opens the eustachian tube, thereby providing a path between the middle ear and the outside world, permitting this pressure equalization to take place. The reason stewardesses used to pass out chewing gum on airplanes was to help passengers keep their eustachian tubes open with the chewing and swallowing movements. If pressure in the middle ear were to remain constant and outside air pressure were to change rapidly, considerable discomfort would result, and a large enough pressure difference could actually cause the eardrum to rupture. The congestion and inflammation that accompanies a cold or sore throat prevents the eustachian tube from opening properly. Thus people who have a cold are more likely to experience discomfort when flying or when exposed to other sources of fluctuation in atmospheric pressure.

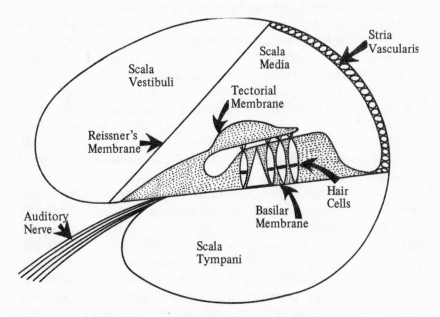

Figure 6. Cross section through the human cochlea.

The Inner Ear

The major auditory structure in the inner ear is the *cochlea*. The cochlea is a bony structure having the shape in man of a snail shell with 2 1/2 coils. As depicted in Figures 6 and 7, the cochlea is composed of three fluid-filled canals called the *scala vestibuli*, the *scala tympani*, and the *scala media*. These canals are filled with an incompressible fluid. Careful observation of Figure 7 shows that the scala vestibuli and the scala tympani are actually connected at the tip or *apex* of the cochlea. The opening at the apex of the cochlea that connects these two canals is called the *helicotrema*. The middle canal, or scala media, is isolated from the upper and lower canals by *Reissner's membrane* on the top, and the *basilar membrane* on the bottom.

The actual sensory receptors for hearing, called *hair cells,* are contained in a structure known as the *organ of Corti,* located on the basilar membrane. There are approximately 23,500 hair cells on the bisilar membrane of each cochlea. As shown in Figure 6, the tips of the hair cells are in physical contact with a stiff structure projecting over them, known as the *tectorial membrane.* The arrangement of the hair cells and the tectorial membrane is such that an up and down movement of the basilar membrane would cause the hair cells to be bent against the tectorial membrane. A mechanical bending of the hair cells against the tectorial membrane is actually the event that results in our perception of sound. When sheared against the tectorial membrane, the hair cells release a chemical substance that leads to the generation of electrical impulses in the auditory nerve.

As is shown in Figure 7, two membrane covered openings, the *oval window* and the *round window,* separate the scala vestibuli and scala tympani from the middle ear. Note that the foot plate of the stapes fits into the oval window. Vibration of the eardrum causes the foot plate of the stapes to move the oval window in and out. Because the scala vestibuli and the scala tympani contain an incompressible fluid (known as perilymph) and because of the opening (helicotrema) which connects the

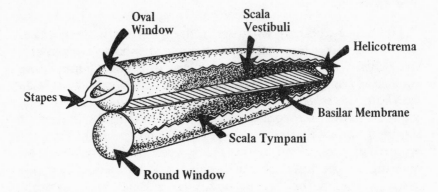

Figure 7. Cut-away view of the cochlea as it might appear if it could be uncoiled. Note the change in width of the basilar membrane as it proceeds from base to apex.

scala vestibuli and the scala tympani, the round window is forced outward when the oval window is pushed inward by the foot plate of the stapes. Thus, vibrations of the eardrum start a chain of events which causes the perilymph to move back and forth over the scala media. This back and forth movement of the perilymph produces an up and down movement of the basilar membrane, resulting in the hair cells being bent or sheared against the tectorial membrane.

The physical characteristics of the basilar membrane, which is 27 millimeters long in the human, are such that it is narrow (.04 millimeters) and stiff at the end of the cochlea near the oval window (called the basal end), and it becomes progressively wider and less stiff as it proceeds toward the apex of the cochlea near the helicotrema. At the apex of the cochlea, the basilar membrane has increased its width to 0.5 millimeters and has decreased in stiffness by a factor of 100. Anyone who has played a stringed instrument knows that a thin, taut string produces a high frequency sound when struck, while a thick, loose string produces a lower pitched sound when struck. In a sense, the basilar membrane may be likened to a guitar string with a continuously increasing thickness and decreasing tautness as it proceeds from base to apex of the cochlea.

These physical properties of the basilar membrane are such

that different frequencies of vibration at the eardrum, when transmitted to the oval window, will produce maximal up and down movement at different points along the length of the basilar membrane. High vibration frequencies will produce maximal displacement at the thin stiff basal end of the membrane, while progressively lower frequencies of vibration will produce maximal displacement farther and farther down the basilar membrane toward the apex of the cochlea. Since high frequency sounds produce high frequency vibration of the eardrum and low frequency sounds produce low frequency vibration of the eardrum, a kind of sound frequency analysis is actually performed in the cochlea due to the physical characteristics of the basilar membrane. High frequency tones result in stimulation of hair cells at the basal end of the cochlea, while low frequency tones stimulate hair cells more toward the apical end of the cochlea. These different populations of hair cells in turn produce electrical excitation in different portions of the auditory nerve, so that different sound frequencies are segregated in different nerve fibers and are transmitted to different parts of the brain.

The above discussion presents a simplified (believe it or not) description of how vibration of the eardrum, produced by disturbances in the surrounding air molecules, leads to back and forth motion in the perilymph and eventually to bending of auditory hair cells against the tectorial membrane. Obviously, it requires less energy to vibrate an object in air than is needed to vibrate an object in a viscous fluid such as perilymph. Yet there seems to be no loss in transmission efficiency from the eardrum, which vibrates in air, to the oval window, which must vibrate against the perilymph. How can this be the case? Recall that the eardrum is approximately 65 square millimeters in surface area, while the oval window is only around 3 square millimeters in surface area. Thus we have a situation where the vibrational force from one structure is being transmitted to another structure only one-twentieth its size. In such a situation, a mechanical amplification process takes place so that the force operating on the oval window is twenty times greater than it would be if the eardrum and the oval window were the

same size. The situation is somewhat similar to the phenomenon that occurred in women's fashions some years ago. At
that time, narrow spike-heeled shoes were in style. However, it
was soon discovered that an average-sized woman wearing such
shoes could actually poke holes in a tile floor. The same
woman wearing conventional heels would do absolutely no
damage to the floor. Her weight is of course the same in both
cases, but it was being focused onto a smaller surface in the case
of the spiked heels. Without the twenty to one size difference
between the eardrum and oval window, our hearing would be
twenty times less sensitive than it is. This twenty to one size
difference between the ear drum and the oval window just
compensates for the fact that perilymph is approximately
twenty times as dense as air and produces around twenty times
as much impedance to a vibrating object.

Physical Changes

All of the above information is intended to serve as a background so that we can more clearly understand those changes
in auditory sensitivity that appear to be associated with the
aging process. Indeed, there is considerable evidence that auditory abilities decrease as a function of age. However, the size of
this decrease is not as great as it was once believed to be. It is
now known that in hearing tests the personality characteristics
of the individual being tested can actually influence the measure of hearing sensitivity that is obtained. One phenomenon
that is associated with aging, not directly related to sensory
abilities, is a tendency for older people to be more conservative.
Apparently older people become more cautious in their actions
due to an increased fear of failure. The elderly seem to value
accuracy over speed; thus in an audiometric test when a tone is
presented that is hardly perceptible, a young person, less cautious about being correct, might report to the audiologist "I
hear it." However, an older person presented with a barely
perceptible tone is less likely to make the response "I hear it,"
preferring to wait until they are quite certain they did in fact
hear a tone. Also, older people seem to have more difficulty in

concentrating on the rather tedious detection task involved in having hearing tested.

Even allowing for these nonsensory "personality" factors, it is still clear that auditory acuity does experience a decline with age. For example, it has been demonstrated that the ability to hear another person whispering falls off measurably with age. A whispered message that could be detected at or beyond 10 meters by persons under 50 years of age could only be heard at a distance of 8 to 10 meters by persons aged 51 to 55, at a distance of 6 to 8 meters by ages 56 to 60, at 3 to 5 meters by ages 66 to 70, and at distance of only 1 to 4 meters by persons over the age of 70.

Some of the physical changes that take place in the auditory system with age have been identified. Let us look at some of these physical changes and discuss their potential for reducing hearing sensitivity.

The Outer Ear

EXTERNAL AUDITORY MEATUS: The meatus, or ear canal, has been shown to change its physical characteristics in the aged. There is actually a reduction in the size of the opening of the canal in the elderly, due to degenerative changes in the cartilage in the canal wall. This would reduce the ability of air molecules in the canal to be activated by sound sources in the environment. Also, particularly in the older male, there is a tendency for coarse hairs to grow around the opening of the ear canal. In some cases, these hairs can actually interfere with hearing sensitivity.

TYMPANIC MEMBRANE: Changes in the thickness and stiffness of the tympanic membrane (eardrum) have been noted in the aged. Such changes would alter the vibratory characteristics of the eardrum and result in a change in hearing sensitivity.

Temporal Bone

As indicated in Figure 5, the cochlea is encased in the temporal bone of the head. The method of sound transmission that we have been discussing so far, where air molecules displace the eardrum, is referred to as *air conduction*. Vibrations from a sound source also reach the cochlea by another means known as *bone conduction*. Sound waves actually set up vibrations in the temporal bone; through the mechanism of bone conduction, these vibrations produce excitation of the auditory hair cells and result in the perception of sound. Ordinarily, we perceive sounds both by way of air conduction and by bone conduction. However, these two mechanisms are not equivalent in their ability to transmit high and low frequency sounds. Air conduction favors high frequency sounds, whereas bone conduction favors the transmission of low frequency sounds. This distinction between air conduction and bone conduction is the reason most people are surprised (and usually disappointed) the first time they hear themselves speak on a tape recorder. We are used to hearing our own voice through both air conduction and through the vibrations set up in the temporal bone (bone conduction). When we hear ourselves over a tape recorder, the bone conduction component of the sound is significantly reduced because the sound source is no longer the internally located vocal cords but the externally located tape recorder speaker. Since the tape recorder is farther away from the temporal bone than are the vocal cords, we usually perceive our own voice over a tape recorder as being too high pitched and nasal sounding because the lower, more resonous pitches usually mediated by bone conduction are being selectively reduced. Yet, the way we sound over a tape recorder is actually the way that we always sound to other people. The contribution of bone conduction to hearing our own voice can be experienced by listening to ourselves talk with our ears plugged up. Now, we perceive our voice as being deep and rich sounding, because the high frequency components of our voice mediated by air conduction are being prevented from reaching the eardrum; we are listening to ourselves only through bone conduction.

Normal hearing through bone conduction depends upon the physical characteristics of the temporal bone. The temporal bone (and bone in general) is not a lifeless substance as it may appear to be. Rather, bone is living tissue that is constantly being destroyed and replaced by the body. In old age, there is a tendency for bone to degenerate and to be reabsorbed by the body faster than new bone is formed. This is why broken bones are more serious in the elderly than in young people. In some elderly people a condition known as *senile osteoporosis* exists, where the bones become very fragile and porous. These bones are highly susceptible to fracture. When such a condition occurs in the temporal bone it can have negative consequences for hearing by producing a loss of bone conduction for low frequencies. Although the exact causal mechanism remains unclear, there is some evidence that there is a relationship between one's level of physical activity, estrogen levels, and osteoporosis. It seems that less physically active people are more apt to develop senile osteoporosis, as are menopausal women whose estrogen levels have decreased.

The Middle Ear

The middle ear contains the malleus, incus, and stapes (ossicles) which are critical structures for transmission of sound by way of the air conduction route. There is little that has been discovered to date that attributes changes in the middle ear to the aging process *per se*. However, at any age middle ear infections or other accumulations of fluid in the middle ear will interfere with air conduction by inhibiting free movement of the ossicles. Thus, colds and sore throats should be carefully monitored to insure that the eustachian tube does not serve as a passageway by which infections in the throat can invade the middle ear.

Another source of hearing loss that involves the middle ear is the condition known as *otosclerosis*. In otosclerosis, a soft, bony growth forms at the point where the foot plate of the stapes fits into the oval window. As this bony growth develops, the mechanical transmission of vibrations from the ossicles to the auditory hair cells in the cochlea is impeded. Otosclerosis severe enough to cause hearing loss has been estimated to occur in approximately one percent of the white population of the United States. Otosclerosis seems to have a hereditary basis, tending to appear with greater frequency in some families than in others. The onset of hearing loss associated with otosclerosis is relatively slow. The loss may not be noticeable until the affected individual is well into adulthood, although fixation of the stapes has been detected in children as young as seven years of age.

One of the early signs of otosclerosis is *tinnitus,* or ringing in the ears. This ringing sound is usually high pitched, like a steam whistle, and may be especially noticeable at night or in a quiet environment. Other diagnostic signs of otosclerosis include (1) a history of hearing loss in the family that cannot be accounted for by ear infections; (2) normal appearance of the tympanic membrane; (3) hearing loss that becomes progressively worse; and (4) hearing test results that show impaired air conduction with equal losses at all frequencies, while bone conduction thresholds remain normal. Otosclerosis initially affects only air conductive hearing; however, there will eventually be a loss of both air conductive and bone conductive hearing as the condition becomes worse and nerve deterioration is added to the mechanical problem.

Otosclerosis can be temporarily dealt with by a surgical procedure that involves entering the middle ear through the eardrum and freeing the stapes by fracturing the bony growth attaching it to the oval window. However, this procedure is only effective for a period of several months, after which the bony growth will resume formation. A more effective treatment is the *plantinectomy* procedure, where the foot plate of the stapes is surgically removed and is replaced by a piece of vein from the back of the hand, which will not attach itself to the bone surrounding the oval window. Air conductive hearing is then permanently restored to its normal level.

The Inner Ear

STRIA VASCULARIS: Referring once more to Figure 6, we can see that the outer wall of the scala media is lined with a thin layer of tissue known as the stria vascularis. The stria vascularis, so named because of its rich vascular supply, constantly produces a +80 millivolt DC electrical potential. This "standing DC potential" seems to act as a battery to increase the electrical response that is generated and sent to the brain when the auditory hair cells are sheared against the tectorial membrane. Animal experiments indicate that hearing sensitivity is impaired when the standing DC potential is reduced or abolished by cutting off the blood supply to the stria vascularis. Degenerative changes have been seen in the stria vascularis of human cochlear material obtained from deceased elderly people. These signs of atrophy *may* be related to reductions in the size of the standing DC potential which could contribute to reduced auditory sensitivity in elderly people thus affected.

ORGAN OF CORTI: In the cochlea, the structure located on the basilar membrane containing the auditory hair cells is the organ of Corti. Degenerative changes in the organ of Corti have been seen, especially at the basal end of the cochlea, in tissue samples taken from elderly cadavers. You may recall the discussion of the physical properties of the basilar membrane and how these physical properties cause different populations of hair cells to be stimulated by high and low sound frequencies. It was mentioned that because of its narrowness and stiffness at the basal end, high frequency sounds are maximally effective in stimulating hair cells at this end of the structure. Since the basal portion of the organ of Corti shows degenerative changes as a function of age, one might expect that hearing for high frequencies might be especially susceptible to impairment in older people. Indeed, a hearing loss especially severe for the high frequencies is consistently reported for elderly people. This condition is so common that it is given its own name, *presbycusis*. By age fifty, most people will show a measureable deficit in hearing for tones above 4000 Hz. By age sixty, hearing for tones above 8000 Hz is essentially abolished. Fortunately, most important human speech sounds are made up of frequencies well below 4000 Hz; while presbycusis may prevent an older person from enjoying all of the benefits of an expensive stereo high fidelity record player, this high frequency hearing loss will not significantly interfere with ongoing daily activities.

It is well documented that prolonged exposure to loud noise can permanently reduce hearing sensitivity. One might question whether the decreased sensitivity of the auditory system associated with advancing age may be due at least in part to the fact that older people have been subjected for a longer period of time to the noises associated with our industrialized society. Even listening to a loud power lawn mower for too long has been shown to produce some degree of hearing loss, and many noises that we are exposed to are significantly louder than this. Cross-cultural investigations have been conducted to assess the contribution of modern "noise pollution" to the phenomenon of presbycusis. Measurement of the hearing levels of more primitive (noise-free) societies in Africa and in the Sudan indicate that there is a progressive loss of hearing for high frequencies as a function of age in noise-free societies just as there is in industrialized societies. These findings suggest that presbycusis is primarily an age-related phenomenon, not simply a consequence of long term noise exposure.

While cross-cultural studies indicate that environmental noise is not the major cause of presbycusis, there are environmental factors which contribute to hearing loss in both young and old individuals. Some of these factors will be mentioned since they seem to produce a greater loss in older listeners.

Many occupations involve on-the-job exposure to loud noise, and in earlier times, people who entered these occupations accepted the fact that in future years they would suffer hearing impairment. The term "boiler maker's deafness" grew out of the observation that individuals who worked in a boiler factory would eventually show signs of deafness as a result of constant exposure to the loud noise. Today, however, labor union contracts as well as governmental regulations require that industrial noise levels be kept below the hazardous range, and "noise pollution" equipment such as ear plugs, ear muffs, or sound shielding material is used to combat job-related hearing loss. Hearing sensitivity of workers in various occupations is also measured periodically to determine where precautions against noise-induced hearing loss are inadequate. Such measurements have indicated that older workers show a greater susceptibility to noise damage than do younger workers. Young and old workers who initially have comparable hearing levels for pitches in the lower and middle frequency ranges show differential effects after exposure to industrial noise. It is true that anyone who target-shoots, hunts, or works in a noisy environment should take precautions against excessive noise exposure; it is especially critical that older individuals take such precautions, because they appear to be particularly vulnerable to noise-induced hearing loss.

The kinds of cross-cultural observations mentioned earlier provide another indication that environmental noise makes a contribution to the hearing loss seen in older people. Both elderly men and women show signs of presbycusis in all societies; however, in industrialized societies, older men show a significantly greater hearing loss than older women. This sex difference in hearing loss is small or absent in nonindustrialized societies. In industrialized societies, men are more likely than women to be employed in occupations that involve excessive noise exposure, and in such societies men eventually show a significantly greater hearing loss than women.

An additional environmental factor that can be related to hearing loss is the use of certain antibiotics. It has been known for some time that some antibiotic drugs such as streptomycin can produce a permanent hearing decrement. In fact, streptomycin has been used in animal experiments expressly for the purpose of reducing auditory sensitivity. In sufficient concentrations, streptomycin can destroy the auditory hair cells on the basilar membrane. This, in turn, produces an irreversible hearing loss. There seems to be a cumulative effect of certain antibiotics on auditory hair cells, so that prolonged exposure even to normal doses of streptomycin can eventually have harmful consequences for hearing. This means that older people, who are generally more susceptible to various illnesses and infections than younger people, should be aware that prolonged use of certain antibiotics involves the risk of auditory hair cell damage. We will discuss drugs that can be harmful to hearing more fully in a later chapter.

Perceptual Changes

Perhaps the most significant function of the human auditory system is its ability to receive and process information in the form of speech sounds. Many lower animals including insects, birds, and fish use different sounds to communicate specific messages. However, no animal language even begins to approach the complexity and versatility of human speech. We have been discussing the fact that by age sixty there is a general impairment for all sound frequencies, with the losses being especially severe for tones of 4000 Hz and higher. Thus it might be expected that some decrement in speech comprehension would occur due to the aging process. Indeed, studies have indicated that older listeners show poorer ability than younger listeners in the discrimination of speech sounds. Interestingly, the losses in speech comprehension seen in older people are greater than would be predicted from the losses seen in their performance with simple tones of different frequencies. This has led some investigators to speculate that speech-sound-hearing losses may occur due to involvement of higher auditory brain structures that have not been discovered as yet, rather than just to middle ear and/or cochlear changes.

Ordinarily, the deficit in speech-sound perception in an older person develops as a gradual process, and the affected individual may be unaware that any change in his or her auditory sensitivity is taking place. The gradual onset of age-related hearing loss and the accompanying decrement in speech comprehension can sometimes result in personality changes. A dramatic example of such a change is the phenomenon sometimes referred to as "paranoia of the deaf." In this situation, the older person suffering the hearing loss may come to believe that people are talking about him or her, since they seem to be talking in muffled tones to keep him or her from overhearing the conversation. What has happened, of course, is that people are talking at the same level that they always used, but the affected individual is now unknowingly operating with a reduced level of auditory sensitivity. Unfortunately, these feelings of paranoia may produce a change for the worse in the affected individual's interactions with other people, which leads to a vicious circle by in turn causing other people to react in a more negative fashion to the person exhibiting the paranoia.

Suggestions

A recognition of the fact that hearing loss generally accompanies advancing age can help a person to prepare, both physically and psychologically, for this eventuality. There are some simple precautions that should be taken to insure that hearing loss is kept to a minimum.

Prolonged exposure to loud noise should be avoided by both young and old, but especially by the old. Participating in regular physical activity seems to be beneficial, since it may help to keep the bones of the body, including the temporal bone, from becoming brittle and porous; in addition, exercise may prove to be of value to the blood vessels of the stria vascularis.

Periodic audiometric examinations especially after the fifth decade of life can keep one posted as to the overall state of the auditory system. One should keep in mind that there is no disgrace in asking a speaker to talk a little louder. In some instances, the use of a hearing aid can be quite beneficial for both air conductive and bone conductive hearing losses. People appear to be relatively accepting of the fact that they cannot run as fast, jump as far, or lift as much in old age as they could in their youth; they adjust their activities and their expectations accordingly. A healthy approach to age-related hearing loss would be to similarly recognize and compensate for, to the greatest extent possible, the changes that will occur in the auditory system.

Chapter 4

THE VESTIBULAR SYSTEM

THE structures comprising the vestibular system are located in the inner ear, quite close to the cochlea. The vestibular system is usually referred to as our "sense of balance," although actually, the vestibular apparatus serves two quite different functions. One portion of this system, the *semicircular canals*, are designed to detect changes in acceleration and deceleration; another portion of the vestibular system, the *utricle* and *saccule*, provide us with information about the orientation of our head with respect to the direction of the earth's gravitational force.

These two components of the vestibular system are depicted in Figure 8. We will talk about the semicircular canals first. Each inner ear contains three semicircular canals. While it is difficult to depict their three-dimensional arrangement in a two dimensional drawing, Figure 8 attempts to show that the three canals are pointed in different directions and are situated almost at right angles to one another.

Each canal is filled with an incompressible fluid known as endolymph (this is the same fluid found in the scala media of the cochlea). Movement of the body in any direction will produce movement of this endolymph, just as movement of your body would cause displacement of the coffee in a cup that you were carrying. Movement to your left would cause the coffee to splash toward the right. The amount of displacement of the coffee would be determined by the suddenness and vigor of your movement. Similarly, the amount of displacement of the endolymph in the semicircular canals is dependent on the velocity of body movement. Because the semicircular canals are aimed in different directions, movements of the body in the forward or backward direction, or to the left or right, will result

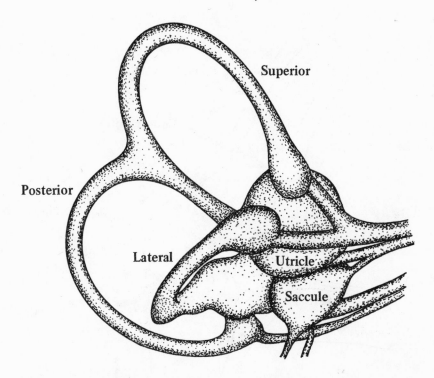

Figure 8. Semicircular canals, utricle, and saccule in the right inner ear. A symmetrically arranged set of structures is located in the left inner ear.

in the fluid displacement in one canal being greater than fluid movement in the other two. Thus, we can tell in which direction we are moving even with our eyes closed, because our semicircular canals are differentially sensitive to movement in different directions.

Note in Figure 8 that there is a prominent bulge at the base of each semicircular canal. This bulge, called the *ampulla,* contains a flexible structure known as the *cupula.* The arrangement of the cupula within the ampulla is shown in Figure 9. Note that in the resting position the cupula blocks fluid movement in its particular semicircular canal. When a person moves, the resulting displacement of the endolymph pushes against the cupula and causes it to move laterally. This lateral movement in turn causes bending of tiny hair cells called *cilia*

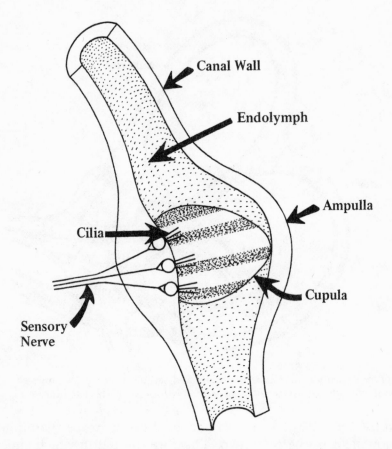

Figure 9. Cross section of ampulla found at the base of each semicircular canal. Note the position of the spring-loaded cupula within the ampulla.

that are imbedded in the base of the cupula. Bending of these hair cells generates electrical impulses that are transmitted to the vestibular portions of the brain, telling us that motion in some direction is taking place.

Because of the physical properties of the cupula, the semicircular canals cannot detect steady-state movement. They can only respond to increases or decreases in our rate of movement. For example, even blindfolded one can readily detect the movement associated with accelerating rapidly in a car from zero to 55 miles per hour. But once you reach and maintain 55 miles per hour, the semicircular canals would no longer be activated because they are not sensitive to a constant rate of speed. However, when you begin to slow down from 55 miles per hour, the semicircular canals would again be affected and you would be aware of the change in velocity.

The reason that the semicircular canals are not sensitive to steady-state movement is because the cupula is "spring-loaded." That is, the initial change in velocity produces a bending of the cupula, but with no further increases in acceleration the cupula will return to its original position in a matter of seconds, blocking the ampulla, and stopping the movement of endolymph. An analogy might be the way a young tree is bent over by a sudden gust of wind; however, even if the wind continues to blow at the same intensity, the tree returns to its original position.

In man, each semicircular canal is sensitive to movement in two opposite directions, depending upon which way the cupula is displaced. The same canal is also involved in detecting both acceleration and deceleration in the same direction. It is of some interest that each canal in the inner ear of a frog is sensitive only to movement in one direction. This suggests that, even if they had occasion to do so, blindfolded frogs would be unaware they were hopping backwards. Their semicircular canals are designed only to detect movement in the forward direction.

As was mentioned above, the utricle and saccule (see **Fig. 8**) make up the gravitational detection portion of the vestibular system. The operation of the utricle and saccule is surprisingly simple. These two structures are lined with sensory hair cells, or cilia. The cilia are covered by a layer of *otoliths,* which are small hard particles of calcium carbonate (the term otolith actually means *ear rock*). These otoliths are imbedded in a jellylike substance into which the tips of the cilia extend. When the head is raised or lowered, its center of gravity changes and the force of gravity causes the otoliths to shift their weight and move the cilia under them. This bending of the cilia in turn leads to the generation of electrical impulses in the vestibular nerve. Unlike the cupula in the semicircular canals, the cilia in the utricle and saccule are not spring-loaded. The cilia in the utricle and saccule remain displaced laterally as long as the head is not perpendicular to the pull of gravity. Our gravitational sense is an exception to the usual finding in sensory systems of adaptation over time. As long as we are off balance, we continue to be made aware of it by the continuous generation of electrical impulses which originate in the cilia.

An interesting demonstration can be performed with a crustacean such as a lobster that shows the way the utricle and saccule operate. The balance organ in the crustacean does not manufacture otoliths as does the vertebrate utricle. Rather, the crustacean depends upon the chance accumulation of grains of sand from its environment to do the job of our otoliths. It is possible to remove the sand grains from the crustacean balance organ and substitute tiny iron filings in their place. Then, using a magnet, it is possible to elicit from the animal various righting movements and attempts to "regain its balance," even though it may be standing perfectly upright. When we position the magnet on one or the other side of the animal we are creating an asymetrical pull on the iron filings, causing a bending of the cilia similar to what would occur if the animal were in fact falling over. The animal makes frantic attempts to right itself, even though these attempts are useless and unnecessary.

A consequence of the way that the utricle and saccule operate is that they provide us with no information in a gravity-free environment. Astronauts training in a gravity-free (zero g) environment are unable to tell up from down if they have their eyes closed or visual cues are otherwise eliminated. The reason for this, of course, is that there is no gravitational force acting on the otoliths, and they do not displace the cilia under them. A related but more serious phenomenon has been observed in the case of scuba divers who are operating in very deep or murky water. Divers have been known to get totally disoriented and actually swim in a downward direction when they mean to swim to surface. The water alters the effects of gravity on their balance organs, and in deep or cloudy water the available visual cues may be insufficient to permit the diver to know which direction is up.

We generally take our gravitational system for granted because righting responses and attempts to regain our balance are reflexive in nature and occur without our conscious awareness. Nevertheless, there are several interesting aspects to the vestibular system that should be mentioned. First, not many people are aware of the fact that the vestibular system is developed and functioning in the human infant quite some time before the visual and auditory systems are operating. Infants are able to recognize their mothers (or any familiar person) by the characteristic way they are held and rocked months before they recognize their mothers by sight alone. A baby is sensitive to whether the person holding it is relaxed and at ease. Babies will fuss and cry when held by a tense person long before they will respond to the sight of a frown or a scowl on a human face.

Some research in the Soviet Union done on premature babies indicates that learning occurs earliest when vestibular stimulation is involved, well before learning will occur in the presence of auditory or visual stimuli. This research made use of the fact that premature infants show a strong sucking reflex when an object touches their lips. The investigators found that if they first rocked the baby and then touched its lips, after several such pairings of rocking and lip touching the baby would make sucking movements when it was rocked even if the lip stimulation was withheld. It had learned that vestibular stimulation (rocking) would be followed by lip stimulation. However, when the researchers paired a tone or a light flash with the lip stimulation, they were not able to elicit the sucking reflex to the tone or light in the absence of lip stimulation until the baby was considerably older. These infants were also seen to be able to tell the difference between up and down rocking and back and forth rocking long before they could make the distinction between a high tone and a low tone, or a red light and a green light.

This research strongly suggests that positional and motional changes in the environment are meaningful to the child before auditory and visual events take on significance. Actually, such a finding becomes more understandable when one stops to consider that vestibular reactions, such as standing up straight or recovering your balance after stumbling, occur reflexly without much conscious thought on our part. This implies that vestibular functions are controlled by more primitive parts of the brain than are reactions to sights or sounds, and the primitive parts of the brain are known to be the earliest to develop. In fact, the righting responses that permit a blind-folded cat to land on its feet when unexpectedly dropped remain essentially intact even when severe damage has been inflicted on the higher (cortical) portions of the cat's brain. When damage is done to the cat's vestibular structures, a blind-folded cat is just as likely to land on its head when dropped upside down.

Another interesting aspect of the vestibular system is its contribution to the phenomenon of motion sickness. Motion sickness, for those individuals fortunate enough not to know, is accompanied by headache, chills, sweating, nausea, and feelings of muscular weakness. These symptoms may persist for some time after the motion has stopped, occasionally lasting several days. The vestibular system is sensitive to two different categories of positional and velocity changes, those produced by the person actively moving (such as walking, bending over, or turning the head), and those changes imposed on the individual by some external source, such as the movement of a car or plane, or the listing of a ship. Evidence suggests that movement or orientational changes imposed on the individual by external forces are much more likely to produce motion sickness than are movements initiated by the individual. In addition, not all externally imposed movements are equally likely to produce motion sickness. Short, rapid movements (possibly because they resemble head and eye movements made by the individual) are less effective than slower oscillations of acceleration and deceleration in eliciting motion sickness. Vertical movements such as those experienced when floating on ocean waves or when riding in the back seat of a car with bad shock absorbers are more likely to produce motion sickness than are lateral movements. There is also a learning component involved in motion sickness. Some individuals who have become sea sick while traveling by ship in the past become conditioned to be ill in the future, and they may actually experience feelings of nausea upon boarding a ship, even before it begins to move.

It is quite clear that stimulation of the vestibular system is involved in motion sickness, in that deaf persons who have had severe damage to the inner ear, leaving them with no vestibular or auditory sensitivity, do not experience motion sickness. People with no vestibular sensitivity are still able to maintain an upright position and move about in a normal fashion, but only with their eyes opened. They have learned to utilize visual cues alone in situations where normal individuals make use of a combination of visual and vestibular information.

Just as is the case with our other senses, there are large individual differences between people in their vestibular sensitivity. For instance, when blindfolded and seated in a specially constructed tilting chair, some people can tell when their bodies have been tilted as little as 2 or 3 degrees from the vertical axis. On the other hand, some people must be tilted as much as 14 degrees before they perceive any tilt at all. As might be expected, the aging process appears to be one causal factor in altering vestibular sensitivity. Some degenerative changes have been noted in the vestibular nerves of elderly persons. Such changes have been implicated in decreased sensitivity to tilt. Another obvious example of a differential response to vestibular stimulation as a function of age can be seen in the case of reaction to oscillating motion such as swinging on a swing. As a general rule, most children like swings, while many adults do not. Not only do many adults not like swings, but a surprisingly large number of adults are actually made ill by swinging on a swing. The number of such adults seems to increase in older segments of the population.

Typically, older persons are more susceptible than younger persons to discomfort induced by swinging. Why should this be the case if the vestibular system of the younger person is actually more sensitive than that of the older person? One explanation that has been proposed for this effect has to do (strangely enough) with changes in the internal organs that occur with age. The stomach muscles lose their tone, fat accumulates, and internal organs are not held in place as firmly in older people as they are in children and young adults. Thus, feelings of discomfort arising from movements of the visceral organs may increase the likelihood of motion sickness in elderly people.

Certain drugs are known to have harmful effects on the vestibular system, and these negative effects appear to be more common in the elderly. There are of course the well-known effects of alcohol on balance and coordination. These effects are reversible and wear off when the alcohol has been metabolized and leaves the system. However, there are some drug effects that are far more serious in that they are irreversible. Earlier it was mentioned that certain antiobiotics such as streptomycin can poison the auditory hair cells and cause hearing loss. The same circumstance can occur with the cilia of the vestibular system. Streptomycin has been shown to be related to degenerative changes in the vestibular system, as have certain diuretic drugs. As elderly persons are more likely to be afflicted by medical conditions that require treatment with antibiotics or diuretics, they are more likely to experience these unfortunate vestibular changes.

A relationship also appears to exist between hypertension (high blood pressure) and the vestibular system. A significant number of hypertensive patients report spells of dizziness, and some physicians recognize the possibility that hypertension in some way damages the cilia in the vestibular system. Of course, hypertension is a condition that is not restricted to the elderly, but it is more likely to be found in the elderly.

To summarize briefly, information about the orientation and movement of our bodies in space is provided by the vestibular system. Changes in our ability to process this information seem to occur as a function of age, although some of these changes can be kept to a minimum if a person stays in good health and in good physical condition. In such individuals, hypertensive changes in the circulatory system are minimized, stomach muscle tone is maintained so that the visceral organs are more firmly held in place, and prolonged use of antibiotic or diuretic drugs is less likely to be required.

Chapter 5

THE OLFACTORY SYSTEM

PEOPLE tend to think of the sense of smell as our least important sense modality. It is generally felt that one could lose one's sense of smell and hardly miss it. Actually, our sense of smell is probably more acute and more important than we realize. While human beings are more dependent on sight and sound, the sense of smell does have some protective functions. We are able to detect the odor of smoke, as well as the odor of harmful chemicals such as sulphuric acid. We can also detect spoiled foods by their characteristic unpleasant odor, even when they may look perfectly edible.

From an evolutionary perspective, the importance of the sense of smell is obvious. Many lower organisms have no hearing, and many have no light sensitivity, but there is no living organism that does not react to chemical stimuli. Many lower animals use the sense of smell to seek mates, to distinguish friend from foe, and to find food. Even the single-celled amoeba is able to chemically distinguish between edible and inedible material.

In higher animals such as vertebrates, chemical sensitivity has evolved into two separate sensory systems, smell (or olfaction) and taste (or gustation). These two systems have separate receptors, separate nervous pathways, and separate brain regions. Some indirect evidence suggesting that the sense of smell is more important than most people believe is seen in the fact that twenty different regions of the human brain appear to receive inputs from the smell receptors.

The human olfactory system is depicted in Figure 10. The actual receptors for smell are located high in each side of the olfactory cleft on a 2.5 square centimeter piece of tissue called the *olfactory epithelium*. The stimuli for smell are airborne gasseous particles. The olfactory epithelium has a yellowish

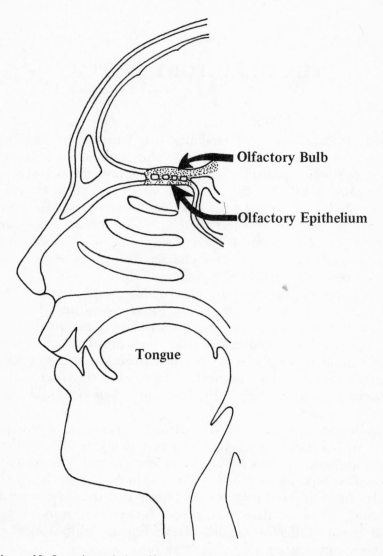

Figure 10. Location of the olfactory receptors on the olfactory epithelium. Receptors are not in the direct path of inspired air and are reached only by eddy currents.

brown hue in normal individuals. This color is apparently produced by a yellow pigment that is necessary for normal olfactory perception. The importance of this yellow pigment is indicated by the fact that human albinos who lack the pigment are also lacking in olfactory sensitivity.

Each receptor cell on the olfactory epithelium contains up to 1000 hairlike filaments to help trap molecules of the odorous substance. The olfactory epithelium is situated in the nose in such a manner that it is not in the direct path of air inspired through the nose. Rather, olfactory stimuli reach the olfactory epithelium by way of eddy currents that are set up after a "sniff" has occurred. Thus, sniffing is a good way to increase smell sensitivity. The olfactory receptors are extremely sensitive, yet they are known to fatigue quite rapidly. At one extreme we are able to detect the odor of a single drop of perfume diffused into a three-room apartment when we first arrive on the scene. At the other extreme, after ten minutes of exposure the odor of a riding stable is hardly noticeable.

Compared with our other senses, little research has been concerned with olfaction. This is undoubtedly due to such factors as the inaccessibility of the olfactory receptors, the generally held belief that smell is not very important, and problems of controlling the stimulus (you cannot simply turn a smell on and off as you can a light or a tone). This lack of basic research in smell is evidenced by the rather imprecise vocabulary used to describe olfactory sensations. We can specify in considerable detail the color of an object by referring to its wavelength in nanometers, or the pitch of a sound by measuring its frequency in cycles per second; but the vocabulary used to describe smells is composed of such vague descriptive terms as "fruity," "burnt," or "putrid," and quantitative units of measurement are entirely lacking. Actually, we are not even certain what physical characteristics of a substance give it a particular smell, although one widely held theory of smell is the "molecular configuration" theory. This theory proposes that the smell of a substance is determined by the physical shape of its molecules. Different smell receptors are thought to have different shaped sites on their surfaces that are best fit by different shaped molecules, just as a given lock is best fit by a particular shape of key. Some support for this lock and key type theory of smell is found in the fact that bringing about a small alteration in the molecular configuration of a substance can cause a significant change in the odor of the substance.

It is now fairly clear that some changes in olfactory perception occur at different times in our lives. Some of these changes are the result of learning, some the result of cultural factors, and some the result of the aging process.

Our society actually teaches its members to under use their sense of smell. For instance, children will naturally attempt to smell a strange food on their dinner plate before putting it in their mouths, and the mother's typical response to this is something like "don't smell your food, it's bad manners." Children (and adults) are constantly exposed to endless commercials on radio and television for soaps, deodorants, room sprays, and other products designed to remove olfactory stimuli from the environment. Such propaganda leads to the belief that human beings are not, and should not be, olfactory creatures. The fact that most of us under use our sense of smell is demonstrable when we look at the olfactory abilities of people who do not have the use of their eyes and ears. Helen Keller, for instance, was reported to be able to recognize her acquaintances on the basis of their smell. The implication here is that if we were forced to, we could learn to make greater use of our sense of smell. Certain non-Western societies are actually able to distinguish other nationality groups on the basis of their smell. The Chinese, for example, sometimes report that Western people have an unpleasant odor about them. This odor is apparently related to the dietary differences between the two cultures.

In addition to being more sensitive than most of us realize, there are olfactory components to various behaviors that we may not be aware of. Let us look at some examples of behaviors that might be influenced by alterations in our sense of smell.

MENTAL IMAGERY: Some people possess very vivid mental imagery. They are able to voluntarily evoke a mental image that is in some cases rich in color, detail, and overall realism. While visual imagery is the most common form of mental imagery, some people exhibit a high degree of olfactory imagery. In such people, a particular odor can evoke a very strong recollection of an earlier experience. For one such individual, the characteristic smell of automobile air conditioning evokes the memory of a car trip to Florida taken years ago. A young woman still experiences a mild sensation of nausea when exposed to the odor of turkey soup. This nausea is related to the memory of a bout of morning sickness experienced eleven years earlier when she was preparing a pot of turkey soup. Thus it appears that, at least in some people, the sense of smell is involved in the long-term storage of certain memories.

SENSORY ENHANCEMENT: The interaction between smell and taste is quite well known. Many substances owe a considerable portion of their characteristic "flavor" not to the taste buds but to the olfactory system. The gustatory pleasure of roast turkey, mashed potatoes and gravy, and buttered corn on the cob is significantly reduced if the nostrils are pinched and olfactory input is eliminated. Less well known is the fact that smell also interacts with other sense modalities in producing a characteristic perception. The burning of incense in order to bring about olfactory enhancement of a religious or mystical experience is quite common. Visual and auditory stimuli are known to have been enhanced in two movies that were made with "scent tracks" as well as sound tracks. At various times during these movies, odors were introduced into the theater appropriate to the action taking place on the screen. The odors utilized included foods, flowers, liquors, and perfume. More recently, a brand of T-shirt called Scratch-N-Smell® has been marketed, where the shirt is impregnated with the odor of the object depicted on the front of the shirt; this odor can be released by scratching the object with the fingernail. For instance, a shirt with a lemon on it will give off a lemony odor when the lemon is gently scratched. Scratching the object simply releases molecules of an odorous substance which then become airborne and stimulate the smell receptors on the olfactory epithelium.

Part of the overall feeling of driving a new car appears to come from the characteristic "new car smell" that is present. It is now possible to recapture some of that good feeling without going to the expense of buying a new car. An aerosol spray product is available that delivers a "new car smell" at the press of a button. This product is especially popular with used car dealers.

Just as pleasant situations can be enhanced by olfactory stimuli, it is also the case that unpleasant situations can be enhanced by certain smells. The general feeling of apprehension experienced by many people upon entering the emergency room of a hospital is certainly intensified by the characteristic "hospital smell" that is present.

SEX AND OTHER MOTIVATED BEHAVIORS: It has been known for some time that in certain rodents, such as the rat and the hamster, the olfactory system plays an important part in sexual behavior, pup retrieval, nest building, and territorial marking behavior. Male rats with the olfactory bulbs removed show a reduced tendency to mate with a receptive female rate, while female rats with damage to the ofactory bulbs show a reduced tendency to retrieve any of their pups that wander away from the litter (the olfactory bulbs are brain structures that receive information from the olfactory receptors). These findings also hold for gerbils and hamsters. In addition, hamsters and gerbils with olfactory bulb damage show less territorial marking behavior and build less-well-constructed nests for rearing the young than do animals with the olfactory system intact.

Of perhaps greater interest is the fact that smell has now been shown to play a significant role in the sexual behavior of non-human primates. Chemical sex attractants called *pheromones* have been known for years to play a major part in the mating behavior of insects. More recently, pheromones have been identified that are produced and released by female monkeys at different stages of the estrous cycle and that have the ability to increase the level of sexual activity in male monkeys. This finding has caused investigators to speculate that smell may be involved in the sexual activity of all primates, including human beings.

There are now several lines of indirect evidence suggesting a relationship between smell and sexual behavior in human beings. It has been demonstrated that in human females the sense of smell is related to the estrous cycle. There are compounds that can be smelled quite easily around the time of ovulation that are detected much less easily during the progesterone phase of the estrous cycle. There are also substances that can be smelled by adult women that cannot be smelled by males or by girls that have not reached puberty. Some studies also suggest that odor preferences are quite different for sexually mature males and females. Women show a preference for such odors as camphor, menthol, and citronella oil, while men tend to favor the odors of musk, pine, and cedar. This apparent relationship between sex hormones, sexual maturity, and odor sensitivity suggests that smell may be more involved in human sexuality than previously believed.

An additional piece of indirect evidence relating olfaction to sexual behavior was contained in an obscure article which appeared in a local newspaper many years ago. A steel worker was suing the company he worked for because of injuries suffered in an industrial accident. An object fell off an overhead platform, striking the man on the head. The worker's contention was that, following the accident, his food became bland tasting because it had lost its aroma and he no longer had any sexual interest in his wife. The short article was probably published by the paper with tongue in cheek because of the seeming incongruousness of the man's claim. Some unscrupulous persons who claim "whiplash" injuries following minor auto collisions also have been known to claim that their sex lives have been impaired by the accident, hoping to increase the size of the settlement they will receive from the insurance company. Possibly some reporter perceived this steel worker's claim as falling in the same category. However, it should be noted that this claim was made years ago, well before scientists were speculating that there might be a relationship between smell and sex in human beings.

Much of the above discussion has pointed out that olfaction may be of more significance than most of us realize. Anosmia, the inability to smell, clearly renders food bland and tasteless; anosmia may also produce alterations in motivated behaviors such as sexual activity. This is known to be the case for lower animals, including nonhuman primates. It may also be true to some extent for humans. It may even be the case that the same odorous substance can serve as a sexual attractant for different species. For instance, musk is a major ingredient in perfumes, which are used as sex attractants by humans. Musk is also secreted by the male musk-deer as a sex attractant. In light of the above, complete or even partial anosmia takes on greater importance and is certainly worth discussing.

Anosmia occurs when the nasal passage is obstructed and air currents can no longer pass freely over the olfactory receptors. Common sources of obstruction include nasal polyps, acute sinusitis with accompanying pus formation, and swelling of the mucous lining of the olfactory epithelium due to hay fever and/or head colds. Evidence also suggests that smoking can be a causal factor in reduced olfactory sensitivity. Other causes of complete or partial anosmia include certain drug reactions, severe blows to the head, surgical trauma, gunshot wounds, tumors, and degenerative conditions of the olfactory nerves.

Clearly, some of the above conditions producing anosmia bear no necessary relation to the age of the individual. However, nerve defects, nasal polyps, and a long history of tobacco smoking are more likely to be contributing factors in anosmia in the elderly. It has also been noted that the yellowish color characteristic of the olfactory epithelium in young, healthy humans is less pronounced in the elderly. This suggests that the yellow pigment needed for normal smell sensitivity may be less abundant in the elderly, resulting in reduced olfactory acuity even in the absence of any disease state.

It is highly unlikely that one can completely prevent age-related reductions in olfactory sensitivity. As was just noted, the reduced amounts of the critical yellow pigment seen in the elderly do not seem to be related to any particular pathological condition. Rather, this phenomenon appears to be a natural consequence of the aging process. However, there are factors contributing to anosmia over which we do have some control. Obviously, if one wishes to retain the sense of smell at its greatest level of sensitivity in old age, there are precautions which should be adopted. In view of the fact that smell enhances other sensory experiences, increases our enjoyment of food, may be involved in long term memory storage for past events, and may play a role in human sexual behavior, these precautions are worth emphasizing.

First, nasal polyps and other obstructions of the nasal passages should be medically dealt with. Also, aside from its other deleterious effects, smoking should be recognized as a potential source of anosmia over which we do have control. In addition, sinus conditions and viral infections should be treated and cleared up as quickly as possible. It should also be noted that excessive exposure to x rays has been shown to produce anosmia. As there is cumulative effect of radiation on living tissue, everyone should be cautious about submitting to unnecessary x rays. Finally, it is hoped that no one needs to be warned to avoid gunshot wounds and severe blows to the head because it might interfere with their sense of smell.

In spite of an obvious air pollution problem, our environment contains a wide variety of olfactory stimuli that are available for our interest and pleasure. An awareness of this fact, along with the realization that the olfactory parts of the nervous system may contribute to activities other than simply detecting odors, should motivate us to avoid conditions or circumstances that could be harmful to our sense of smell.

Chapter 6

THE GUSTATORY MODALITY

BEFORE discussing the gustatory (taste) sense, some elaboration is needed on what we mean by the word *taste*. There are two quite different meanings of this word. One meaning is evident in the everyday usage of the word, for instance when we refer to the fact that our coffee "tastes" great. Actually, this common everyday usage of the word taste encompasses temperature, texture, smell, color, even pain sensations, as well as gustatory sensations. Thus, we say that our food is tasteless when we have a head cold and cannot smell its aroma; we say that lumpy mashed potatoes do not tastes as good as smooth mashed potatoes, and cold soup does not taste as good as warm soup. The characteristic taste of carbonated beverages includes mild pain sensations evoked by the carbonation bubbles stimulating the back of the throat. Flat carbonated beverages do not taste right because these mild pain sensations are missing. One local bar gave up the custom of dying the draught beer green on St. Patrick's day because some of the patrons complained that it tasted funny (even though the green coloring agent had no taste). Not surprisingly, a color-blind patron of this bar could not tell the funny tasting green beer from the regular beer.

The above examples should make it clear that the typical usage of the word *taste* actually involves many more kinds of sensations than we realize. The second meaning of the word *taste* is considerably more restrictive in scope. This restricted usage refers to the sensations of sweet, sour, salty, and bitter which can be experienced only by the gustatory receptors found on the tongue in human beings. (Not all creatures have their taste receptors on the tongue as higher animals do. For instance, certain fish have their taste receptors on the surface of their bodies and can actually taste the water as they swim in it; similarly, flies have taste receptors on their legs and can taste a substance as they walk on it.) The strict usage of the word "taste" is usually found only in the scientific literature dealing with gustation. Many researchers studying the sense of taste believe that sweet, sour, salty, and bitter are the taste primaries, in the same way that red, green, and blue are color primaries in vision. The typical stimulus for sweet is common table sugar or sucrose; for salt, the typical stimulus is sodium chloride; for bitter, it is quinine or caffeine, and for sour, an acid such as dilute hydrochloric acid.

In human beings, the sense of taste is dependent upon *receptors* which are located in the *taste buds*. Taste buds surround the taste *papillae,* the pink raised structures visible on the surface of the tongue. Each papilla is surrounded by a small depression or moat. The taste buds are not uniformly distributed over the surface of the tongue. They are located in the moats of the *fungiform papillae* on the tip of the tongue, in the *folliate papillae* on the sides of the tongue, and in the *circumvallate papillae* on the back of the tongue (see top of Fig. 11). The center of the tongue, being devoid of papillae and taste buds, is actually insensitive to gustatory stimuli. Unlike the papillae, taste buds and taste receptors are not visible to the naked eye.

The relationship between taste papillae, taste buds, and taste receptors is depicted in the lower portion of Figure 11. For the sake of simplicity, only one taste bud is shown in this figure. In actuality, there are several taste buds associated with each papilla. The taste buds are made up of clusters of twenty to twenty-five cells in the shape of a goblet. Taste buds contain two different types of cells. Each bud contains several slender, centrally located receptor cells, as well as the thicker, more numerous *sustentacular* or supporting cells. The receptor cells have hairlike projections at their tips which apparently help trap molecules of the substance to be tasted after the substance has flowed into the moat surrounding the papilla. Only substances that go into solution (dissolve in water or saliva) can be tasted. Glass for instance, is insoluble and is therefore tasteless.

After entering into solution and flowing into the moat of a

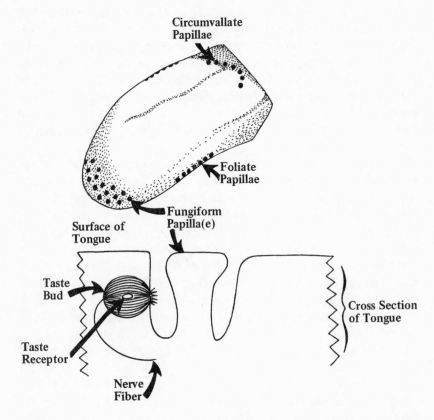

Figure 11. The upper part depicts the location of taste papillae on the surface of the tongue. The lower part shows the relationship between a taste papilla, taste bud, and taste receptor.

papilla, molecules of the taste substance are apparently adsorbed (bonded) to receptor sites on the membrane of a taste receptor cell. This adsorption produces a change in the taste cell's membrane characteristics, permitting the flow of current to occur across the membrane and generating electrical activity in the taste nerves for transmission to the taste centers of the brain.

In addition to providing us with information about our environment, the sense of taste has several other functions. We can detect many potentially harmful substances by their taste. Certain substances elicit pleasurable taste sensations and can actually be used to motivate behavior (for instance, children, dogs, and horses are sometimes manipulated by making use of the "sweet tooth" phenomenon). Finally, there is some evidence that the sense of taste contributes to an animal's ability to choose a nutritionally sound diet.

There seems to be a general tendency in animals to find sweet tastes pleasant and bitter tastes aversive. This tendency does not seem to be based upon learning. Rather, it appears to be instinctive. Various experiments with rats and guinea pigs have shown that animals raised on a bitter tasting diet from birth, never having tasted sweet, still prefer a sweet taste when given a choice later in life. This seemingly innate aversion to the taste of bitter has obvious survival value for an animal living in the wild, since most poisonous substances found in nature have a bitter taste while most sweet-tasting substances are good sources of energy.

Although it is quite widespread, the craving for the taste of sweet (called the sweet tooth) is not universal among all animals. The cat, for example, does not seem to be motivated by the taste of sweet, nor does the chicken. This may be one reason why most circuses contain a trained horse or dog act, but very few contain a trained cat or chicken act. Horses and dogs can readily be rewarded with a lump of sugar or a piece of candy, while cats and chickens cannot be manipulated so easily.

Experiments with nonnutritive substances such as saccharine have shown that it is the sweet taste itself, not the nutritional value of the substance, that is rewarding. In this regard, it is known that electrical messages from the taste receptors on the tongue travel to regions of the brain that do not seem to be directly related to taste. For instance, taste nerve fibers have been shown to project to parts of the *limbic system,* a brain region known to be involved in motivation. Perhaps the preference-aversion properties of sweet and bitter are innately determined by these nerve pathways between the tongue and the limbic system.

The sense of taste is also critical for the appearance of a phenomenon known as "wisdom of the body." This expression refers to the fact that animals (including human beings) seem to actively seek out substances that are needed to maintain their health and well-being. For instance, cows, deer, and other animals actively seek out salt licks, to make up for a lack of readily available salt in their usual sources of food. Failure of these animals to utilize salt licks would result in a sodium deficiency, and eventually in sickness or even death. Similarly, rats that have been raised on a sodium deficient diet or that have had their adrenal glands removed begin taking in abnormally large quantities of salt. Removal of the adrenal gland interferes with (among other things) normal salt metabolism. If an adrenalectomized rat did not take in abnormally large amounts of salt, it would sicken and die. But how do animals know that they have these specific dietary needs? Why are they able to compensate for nutritional deficiencies? The complete answer to this question is not known. However, it is known that the sense of taste is involved, because if the taste system is desensitized such compensation does not occur. If the nerves that carry taste messages from the tongue to the brain are cut, the animal will fail to adequately compensate for a salt deficiency in its diet. Experiments with rats and other animals have shown that, in addition to salt deficiencies, these creatures will also compensate for various vitamin deficiencies by altering their normal food preferences.

The wisdom of the body phenomenon has on occasion been observed in human beings. In one such instance, a young boy developed a strong craving for salt and consumed abnormally large quantities. It was later discovered that the boy had a tumor of the adrenal gland, and that because of adrenal malfunction he actually needed these large amounts of salt for his physical well-being.

As our own experiences have no doubt shown us, the sense of taste shows fairly rapid adaptation. If a strong tasting substance is allowed to remain in the mouth, this adaptation, or decreased taste intensity over time, becomes quite apparent. Adaptation is complete or nearly complete for most substances in from one to three minutes. One interesting consequence of taste adaptation is that we are actually much more sensitive to the taste of salt than we realize. The tongue is constantly bathed in saliva, and saliva contains a low concentration of sodium chloride. This means that our own saliva keeps the taste receptors on the tongue in a chronic state of partial salt adaptation. One easy way to verify this is to dissolve a tablespoon of salt in a glass of water and taste it. Then, stick your tongue out for one minute and allow the saliva on the tongue to dry. Next, taste the salt solution again. The second taste sample should produce a significantly stronger sensation because now your tongue (possibly for the first time in its life) has recovered from saliva adaptation and is now fully sensitive to the taste of salt.

To briefly summarize, there appear to be four primary taste sensations, sweet, salty, sour, and bitter. Sweet seems to be uniformly pleasant to many animals, while bitter seems to be generally aversive. This preference-aversion mechanism does not appear to be the result of learning and may be due to nervous pathways between the tongue and those parts of the brain dealing with motivation. The sense of taste also contributes to the "wisdom of the body" phenomenon. This can be seen in the fact that animals with a dietary deficiency will correct this deficiency by altering their food choices, unless the sense of taste is interfered with.

In keeping with our overall theme, let us now examine some of the changes in taste sensitivity that can be expected to occur as a function of age. As might be expected, there has been relatively little experimental work done on taste changes in the elderly. This is probably because of the widespread belief that taste is not really an important means by which human beings receive information about their environment. Clearly, taste is not as critical as vision or hearing (or perhaps even smell, as we suggested in the last chapter), but it is certainly deserving of greater study than it has received to date. Much of what we believe about human age-related changes in taste is actually based upon extrapolation from experiments dealing with rats, rabbits, and guinea pigs. However, there are some direct observations of human taste changes over time which can be mentioned.

One obvious age-related change in gustation has to do with the number of taste receptors that an individual possesses. In young children, taste buds are found not only on the tongue, but they are also scattered over the insides of the cheeks and pharynx. In adulthood, these extra taste buds have largely disappeared, leaving the tongue as the sole site of gustatory sensation. The presence of extra taste buds and taste receptors may be one reason why the "sweet tooth" phenomenon is generally more pronounced in children than in adults. The children are actually experiencing a greater degree of stimulation from the sweet substance because there are more receptors involved. Of course, children usually have less will power, fewer problems with being overweight (due to their higher activity level), and less concern with "spoiling their appetites" than do adults. Undoubtedly, these nontaste factors also contribute to the strong craving for sweets seen in most children.

In addition to the loss of taste buds and taste receptors from the insides of the cheeks and pharynx, the aging process is associated with a reduction in the number of taste buds and taste receptors on the tongue. It has been estimated that in old age the tongue contains only 50 percent of the taste receptors that were present as a young person. Anatomical studies on the tongue of the rabbit suggest the reason for this reduction in the number of taste receptors. These studies show that taste receptor cells have a relatively short life span and are continually dying off. What appears to happen is that a taste receptor cell dies and is replaced by an adjacent sustentacular (supporting) cell. Upon the death of the receptor cell, a supporting cell moves to a central location in the taste bud and becomes the new taste receptor cell. This turnover process occurs approximately every seven days for each taste receptor. In a young animal, the replacement rate can keep up with the dying off rate. However, in the aging animal, the taste cells continue to have a seven day life span, but the replacement process begins to slow down and eventually falls well behind the dying off rate. The result is that the mature animal begins to experience an irreversible reduction in the total number of taste receptors as compared to the young animal.

While the actual time course may be somewhat different in human beings than it is in rabits, it is quite likely that a similar mechanism is operating in people. This being the case, it would not be surprising to find that changes in taste sensitivity and/or changes in taste preferences occur with advancing age; in fact, the limited evidence available to date suggests that such changes are present. Older people tend to prefer their food with more seasoning and spices than do young children. Presumably this is to compensate for the reduced sensory stimulation that older individuals are receiving from their food. In terms of altered taste preferences with age, there is evidence that the elderly show an increased preference for tart tastes and a decreased preference for sweet. In one of the few studies of human aging and taste preference, subjects were tested with pineapple juice at five different levels of sweetness ranging from tart to sweet. Somewhere between the ages of 50 and 68 there was a clear change in preference toward the tart end of the range and away from the sweet end. In younger persons the preference was toward the sweet end of the continuum.

Some health professionals hold the belief that elderly people who have been heavy smokers for an extended period of time have higher thresholds for some taste substances when compared with elderly people who do not smoke. Here we are probably dealing with an interaction between age and smoking, in that recent evidence has failed to find any reduced taste sensitivity in college students who smoke. While it is anecdotal and has not been scientifically verified, one individual of my acquaintance in his late fifties claims to have lost his sense of taste entirely as a consequence of years of drinking moonshine whiskey (this may not be the complete explanation for his condition).

In addition to the effects of age *per se,* such experiences as exposure to x rays, gunshot wounds, or postsurgical trauma can reduce taste sensitivity. Ordinarily, these changes are reversible.

While on the subject of taste it is appropriate to mention a peripherally related matter, flavor enhancers. Flavor enhancers are substances that are added to foods either during or after preparation to increase the palatability. For instance, a cheaper cut of meat can be made more appetizing by using any of several well-known brands of flavor enhancers. The major ingredient in two of the best known brands of flavor enhancers is monosodium glutamate, more commonly referred to as MSG. It is important to know, however, that different people have different degrees of sensitivity to MSG. For example, not too long ago, a phenomenon was discovered which was called the "Chinese restaurant syndrome." After eating in a Chinese restaurant, some people experienced fever, headache, and feelings of nausea. It has now been determined that these people were experiencing a negative reaction to MSG, which is liberally used in food preparation in some Chinese restaurants. People with an unusually high sensitivity to MSG can still enjoy Chinese food, but they must either choose restaurants that do not use MSG or must call ahead and specially order their meal with the stipulation that no MSG be used in the preparation.

Chapter 7

THE SKIN SENSES

THE skin senses, or *somesthesis,* include sensations of warmth, cold, light touch, pressure, and vibration. Pain is sometimes included under the heading of somesthesis, although we have chosen to deal with pain separately (see following chapter). The skin, which is actually the largest organ of the body, has a surface area of around 2.5 square yards in an average sized adult human. Our skin is the point of interaction between the body and the outside world. The skin provides a protective barrier against potentially harmful objects; the millions of sensory receptors in the skin also enable us to detect such physical characteristics of an object as its roughness or smoothness, hardness or softness, temperature, and wetness or dryness.

The skin is composed of three distinct layers. These are the *epidermis,* the *dermis,* and the *subcutaneous layer.* The outermost epidermal layer is made up of dead cells that are constantly being sloughed off and replaced by an underlying live cell layer. This tendency for skin cells to be constantly sloughed off and replaced is characteristic of people at any age. In fact, it is the basis for the amniocentesis procedure, whereby physicians can test an unborn child for genetic defects as early as the first few weeks of the mother's pregnancy. A sample of the mother's amniotic fluid is withdrawn with a long needle inserted into the abdomen. The chromosomes in skin cells that have been sloughed off by the developing fetus can then be removed from the amniotic fluid and analyzed under a microscope. If genetic abnormalities are discovered, the parents can then undergo counseling to help them cope with a defective child, or the parents may opt for a therapeutic abortion.

Around eighty years ago it became possible for anatomists to microscopically examine human skin samples. The skin was

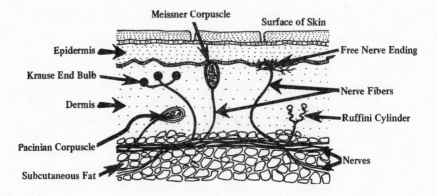

Figure 12. Cross section through the three layers of the human skin.

found to contain three classes of structures: (1) *free nerve endings,* (2) *hair follicles,* and (3) different kinds of sensory receptors that are collectively referred to as *encapsulated end organs.* Figure 12 depicts the different layers of the skin and the three classes of structures found in the skin. Each type of encapsulated end organ has been named after the individual who discovered it. The encapsulated end organs in the skin include Meissner corpuscles, Pacinian corpuscles, Krause end bulbs, and Ruffini cylinders. The encapsulated end organs were thought to be responsible for our sensitivity to warmth, cold, touch, and pressure, while free nerve endings served as pain receptors. More specifically, Krause end bulbs were believed to be cold receptors, Ruffini cylinders were considered to be warm receptors, Meissner corpuscles were presumed to be touch receptors, and the pressure (and later, vibration) receptors were the Pacinian corpuscles.

The beliefs of the anatomists about the functions of the encapsulated end organs were at first apparently supported by the results of experimental studies of skin sensitivity. The skin showed what was called *punctate sensitivity.* That is, not all parts of the skin were found to be equally sensitive to all kinds of test stimuli. A patch of skin on the forearm can be marked (with ink and a rubber stamp) into 1 millimeter grid squares. Then, each square can be tested for its somesthetic sensitivity. One square may be sensitive to touch, but not temperature.

One may be sensitive to warm, but not to cold. An adjacent square may be sensitive to cold, but not warm. Some squares may be completely insensitive, while others may have very high pain sensitivity. Ordinarily, we are unaware of the punctate sensitivity of our own skin because most objects that we come into contact with in our daily lives stimulate an area of skin much larger than one square millimeter.

It was believed by the early anatomists that a "warm" square contained a Ruffini cylinder, a "cold" square contained a Krause end bulb, a "touch" square contained a Meissner corpuscle or a Pacinian corpuscle, and a "pain" square contained a free nerve ending. This relationship between sensory spots on the skin and encapsulated end organs was generally believed until about twenty-five years ago. However, it is now recognized that this simple relationship between a specific encapsulated end organ and specific sensation is not a perfect one. Spots on the skin have been found that are quite sensitive to touch or temperature; yet if the spot of skin is surgically removed and studied under a microscope (some researchers will even give their skin for science) there may be no trace of an encapsulated end organ. Rather, the spot of skin may possess only free nerve endings. Experiments on the cornea of the eye also call into question the earlier view that encapsulated end organs are necessary for the perception of touch and temperature. The cornea of the eye contains only free nerve endings and no encapsulated end organs, presumably so that the passage of light into the eye will be as unobstructed as possible. Yet the human cornea can perceive warmth, cold, and touch as well as pain. Where they exist in the skin, the encapsulated end organs seem to be responsible for touch and temperature sensitivity. However, the evidence suggests that some free nerve endings must also be able to signal touch and temperature, in addition to mediating pain sensitivity.

Touch

As was mentioned earlier, Meissner corpuscles and Pacinian corpuscles are thought to be the receptors for light touch and for pressure. It was also noted that some free nerve endings must be sensitive to touch, as touch spots are found in parts of the skin that contain no encapsulated end organs. The entire surface of the skin is not uniformly sensitive to touch. The finger tips and the lips are much more sensitive to touch than the abdomen or the back. The touch sensitivity of the finger tips is actually quite remarkable when we stop and think about it. We are able to tell (for instance) whether or not we have our car keys in our pocket by feeling for them right through the material of our clothing. We are able to discriminate the difference between the keys, loose change, a book of matches, or any other miscellaneous objects, even through the cloth of the pocket. Try this same discrimination task with the palm of the hand, the back of the hand, and finally with the forearm. The palm provides some minimal information about what is in your pocket, the back of the hand is essentially useless, and the forearm provides absolutely no fine touch discrimination. Actually, with the exception of the lips, touch sensitivity in the body is organized in a manner exactly opposite to the organization of pain sensitivity. Pain spots are greatest in density along the midline axis of the body, showing a reduction as we move out the extremities to the fingertips. Touch sensitivity is greatest in the finger tips, and shows a progressive decrease in sensitivity as we move toward the midline axis of the body. Such an arrangement between touch and pain is a fortunate one; we use our extremities to explore the environment, and if our extremities were overly sensitive to pain, this exploratory function would be impaired. Similarly, the midline axis of the body contains the brain, the eyes, and the vital organs. Thus the midline of the body should be highly sensitive to pain in order to be alerted as rapidly as possible to potentially harmful objects before they can do any damage to these vital structures.

In addition to providing us with sensory information and serving as a vehicle for active exploration of the environment, the sense of touch has other less obvious but equally important functions. Tactile stimulation during infancy seems to be critical for normal growth and development in primates including human beings, as well as in lower mammals. Baby monkeys have been raised in isolation, being denied the physical contact with their mothers that is frequently seen to take place in unrestricted monkey colonies. These monkeys that were deprived of maternal touching, hugging, and grooming as infants grow up to be social misfits. They do not interact normally with other monkeys, they usually fail to mate and produce young upon reaching sexual maturity, and if they should bear young, they fail to raise them properly. Distressingly similar observations have been made on human infants raised in crowded orphanages where there is no regular opportunity for the children to be held and cuddled. The child's nutritional needs may be taken care of, but if the infant fails to have a warm, loving physical contact relationship with a parent-figure during the first year of life, that child is significantly more likely to be maladjusted for the rest of his or her life.

In lower animals like cats and dogs, a failure to receive tactile stimulation during infancy can also have serious consequences. Puppies and kittens that are deprived of the characteristic wrestling and rough and tumble play behavior seen in unrestricted litters show at maturity various learning deficits, a reduced tendency to explore their environment, and an inability to respond appropriately to other dogs and cats.

The importance of tactile stimulation in various kinds of human interpersonal relationships is beginning to be recognized. Various kinds of encounter and sensitivity training groups include touching, feeling, and hugging each other as a basic part of the program. Even in our everyday activities, touch plays a significant role in our dealings with other people. We are careful not to touch a stranger even in a crowded elevator, and we feel compelled to apologize if we should accidentally do so. We may shake hands with a new acquaintance, pat a co-worker on the back, and hug and kiss a dear friend. The kind and amount of tactile interaction is determined by the nature of the relationship.

There is other evidence demonstrating that tactile stimulation has important properties that are not directly concerned with exploring the environment. When we are grief stricken or disappointed, it makes us feel better for some reason to be held and comforted. We experience a warm feeling when we hold hands with a loved one, and we feel elated if in a crowd we can reach out and merely touch a celebrity. Some people can only sleep comfortably if they are covered by a blanket even on a warm night. A sense of well-being is produced by the feel of the blanket on the body surface. Clearly, examples such as these indicate that the sense of touch has more aspects to it than we usually suspect.

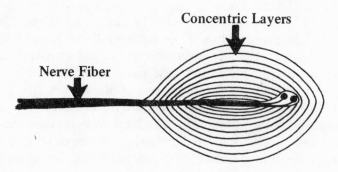

Figure 13. A Pacinian corpuscle with its laminated construction.

Vibration

Vibration is actually the experience of repeated, rapid touch stimulations. It will be recalled that when faint vibrations are rapid enough, and applied to the eardrum, we experience them as sound. The Pacinian corpuscle is the encapsulated end organ in the skin that has been identified as responding to vibration. The Pacinian corpuscle, depicted in Figure 13, has a laminated structure similar to an onion. When the layers of the Pacinian corpuscle are mechanically deformed by some tactile stimulus, the structure responds by generating electrical impulses. These electrical impulses are transmitted to the brain, where they are interpreted as either touch or vibration, depending upon the frequency of stimulation. Electrical recordings made from Pacinian corpuscles in the foot pads of anes-thetized cats show that these structures can respond to vibration rates of several hundred cycles per second.

As is the case with other touch receptors, after a short time the Pacinian corpuscle ceases to be excited by steady state touch or pressure. This phenomenon of adaptation is the reason we are not constantly being stimulated by our watches, rings, and clothing. The touch and pressure receptors under these objects soon adapt to the constant stimulation and stop sending us unnecessary reminders that we are dressed.

Temperature

Just as there are separate touch and pain spots on the skin, so there are separate warm and cold spots. The surface of the human body has been explored with tiny warm and cold probes to map out the distribution of warm and cold spots. A con-sistent finding has been that cold spots are more numerous than warm spots in most body regions. In related experiments subjects have been blindfolded and touched with either a warm or a cold object. The task of the subject is to report the sensa-tion experienced, either warm or cold, as fast as possible. Sub-jects are measurably faster at reporting "cold" than at reporting "warm." Thus it appears likely that cold receptors are located nearer to the skin surface than are warm receptors. Based upon the differential speed of responding to a warm and a cold sti-mulus, it has been estimated that cold receptors are probably 0.1 millimeter deep in the skin and warm receptors are prob-ably located at a depth of around 0.3 millimeters. Interestingly, there do not seem to be separate receptors in the skin for the sensation of "hot." Rather, above temperature of approxi-mately 50°C, both warm receptors and cold receptors are acti-vated. What we perceive as "hot" appears to be the result of simultaneous activation of warm and cold receptor cells. A rather startling effect can be experienced by grasping with the hand a piece of apparatus of the type shown in Figure 14. Two pieces of hollow tubing are coiled and intertwined, one having warm water flowing through it and one having cold water flowing through it. Each of the coils, when touched separately, will feel either warm or cold. But when both coils are touched simultaneously, a strong (though harmless) burning hot sensation is experienced. This effect only makes sense if a hot stimulus is perceived as hot because it produces simultaneous excitation of both warm and cold receptors.

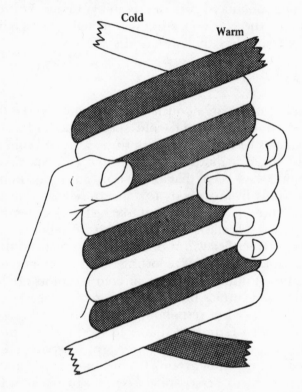

Figure 14. Illusion of burning hot sensation produced by simultaneous warm and cold stimulation.

Fingertip Sight

Another interesting aspect of the skin senses, sometimes referred to as fingertip sight, is worth mentioning. In the past fifteen years, there have been around fifty reports of people who could "see" with their fingertips. One of the more extreme reports came from the Soviet Union, claiming that a young woman wearing a blindfold could "read" the newspaper or describe the pictures on postcards by running her fingers over the paper. This particular report has never been scientifically verified, and a simple explanation for her remarkable ability may be that she was peeking under her blindfold. However, people have been identified who could reliably discriminate different colors of paper with their fingertips. Some of these demonstrations of cutaneous color sensitivity have been performed in carefully controlled laboratory situations with adequate precautions being observed to rule out hoaxing or cheating. How are these people able to perceive color differences with their fingertips? Two possible explanations come to mind. One is that human beings actually possess light-sensitive receptors in the skin, but most of us never use them because we are not aware of their existance. Another possible explanation for cutaneous color sensitivity is that some people have such a sensitive touch system that they can actually discriminate small texture differences that might exist between different colors of paper.

The first possibility has been ruled out by microscopic examination of the skin from human fingertips. There is absolutely no sign of light-sensitive receptors in the skin. The second possibility, that people can discriminate color differences on the basis of texture cues, is ruled out by the ability of some people to discriminate different pieces of colored paper even when the paper is placed under a piece of glass and cannot be directly touched.

The current best guess about cutaneous color sensitivity is that people who demonstrate it are actually responding to very small temperature cues that are associated with different colors of paper. The human body is known to emit infrared radiation, which can be perceived as heat. Light colored paper would tend to reflect this infrared radiation generated by the subject's own hand, and the reflected infrared radiation could then be detected by temperature receptors in the fingertips as a faint temperature increase. Dark colored paper would absorb the infrared radiation from the subject's own hand and the temperature receptors in the fingers might perceive a slight reduction in temperature. This idea is indirectly supported by the fact that even subjects who have a good ability to perceive different colors with their fingertips start out performing only at a chance level, then gradually show improvement with continued practice. Such incremental progress suggests that a learning process is taking place, as the subjects discover through trial and error which colors are associated with which temperature sensations. It is also likely that, in most cases, the learning takes place without the subject even being aware of what he or she is learning. They just find that over time they get better and better at identifying the color correctly.

A few years ago I tested this idea that reflection of infrared radiation may be serving as the basis of cutaneous color sensitivity. Thirty subjects were carefully blindfolded and had their hands placed 1/2 inch above either a normal mirror or a mirror that had been sprayed with a flat black paint. It was felt that the normal mirror would reflect back most of the infrared radiation emitted from the subjects's hands, while the flat black surface would absorb most of the radiation. The subjects were given repeated trials and were asked on each trial whether they were holding their hands over the light or the dark surface. Texture cues were ruled out, as the subjects never actually touched the mirrors. After a series of practice trials during which time they showed a steady improvement, four of the thirty subjects were able to perform consistently above chance (chance was of course 50 percent correct in this two choice situation) in discriminating the light from the dark surface. The remaining twenty-six subjects performed at or around the chance level. Careful questioning of the four successful subjects after the experiment indicated that none of them were aware that temperature cues were probably serving as the basis for their remarkable ability. Just as some people have unusually high visual, auditory, taste, or smell sensitivity, so some people seem to have a highly developed temperature detecting ability.

This extremely fine temperature detecting ability seems to be the basis for the phenomenon of cutaneous color sensitivity.

Age-related Changes in Somesthetic Sensitivity

The vast majority of investigations into the effects of the aging process on sensory abilities have been concerned with the auditory and visual modalities. However, there are some studies of the skin senses that have included a sample of older subjects to compare with the sample of children and young adults. The general conclusion to be drawn from these studies is that there is a decrease in the sensitivity of the skin senses in the elderly. This finding is probably due in part to the fact that the elasticity of aged skin changes, and more pressure is needed to mechanically deform the skin tissue and stimulate the sensory receptors lying beneath the skin. Mechanical deformation is, of course, the necessary stimulus for touch, pressure, and vibration. Anatomists have also reported that there is a decrease in the number of Meissner corpuscles and other encapsulated end organs in the skin of the elderly. This decrease could also contribute to the reduced touch sensitivity noted in older people.

One early study of touch sensitivity showed that the ability to perceive a light touch on the tip of the nose showed a gradual decrease as people increase in age from twenty to fifty, with the decrease in sensitivity becoming quite pronounced for subjects in the eighties. In another experiment with subjects ranging in age from six to eighty-three years, it was reported that the older subjects showed poorer sensitivity to touch on the big toe and fingertip than did the younger subjects. There are also several reports of reduced vibration sensitivity in aged subjects.

The decreases in touch sensitivity reported in the elderly cannot entirely be the result of changes in skin elasticity or reductions in the number of encapsulated end organs. Recall that touch-sensitive spots can be found in the skin independent of encapsulated end organs, and that the cornea of the eye, which has minimal elasticity to begin with, shows touch sensitivity. The cornea also possesses no encapsulated end organs. If all age-related changes in touch sensitivity were due to decreased elasticity and fewer encapsulated end organs, then the sensitivity of the cornea should remain unchanged in the elderly. It does not. Older subjects require a longer duration of air puff to the cornea to perceive the puff when compared with the duration of puff needed by younger subjects. It may be the case that some degree of degeneration of the sensory nerves that carry somesthetic messages to the brain is occurring in the elderly.

There is some evidence in support of this possibility. In a study of the relationship between age and touch sensitivity, human subjects between the ages of three and ninety-six years of age were touched on the cheek, on one or the other of their hands, or on the cheek and one hand simultaneously. The task of the subjects was to report whether they had received one or two touch stimulations on each trial. Children between the ages of three and six, and adults between the ages of sixty-one and ninety-six, had difficulty perceiving and reporting two simultaneous stimulations. They were more likely to perceive only stimulation of the cheek, failing to detect the simultaneous stimulation of the hand. Older children and young adults had no difficulty reporting the two simultaneous touch stimulations. These results suggest that young children had difficulty with the task because their nervous systems were still in an immature state, while elderly people had difficulty because some degenerative changes in their sensory nerves had taken place.

Regarding temperature sensitivity, there is no clear evidence that the elderly become less sensitive to warm and cold stimulation. However, it has been established that they are less able than the young to maintain a constant body temperature when exposed to a hot or cold environment. Younger people have a greater capacity to increase their production of body heat in a cold environment (probably due to a higher basal metabolism rate) and a greater ability to dissipate heat in a warm environment. This is one reason why the elderly are less enthusiastic than the young about skiing on a cold day or playing tennis on a warm one. It is not so much that older people lack the physical capacity for these activities (at least in many cases), but rather that they are subjected to greater temperature-related discomfort and may decide that it is just not worth the effort.

While the above evidence strongly suggests that decreased somesthetic sensitivity occurs in old age, it should be noted that these changes are for the most part small and require controlled experimental situations and weak intensities of stimulation before the changes can even be measured. It appears that, in the absence of pathological conditions such as diseases that produce nervous system degeneration, the changes in touch and vibration sensitivity that may occur with age need not be greeted with fear, and these changes will probably have little if any affect on normal daily activities.

Chapter 8

THE SENSE OF PAIN

PAIN is usually thought to be a fairly simple and straightforward sense that warns us about things in the environment that could cause tissue damage. However, it turns out that pain is really not so simple and straightforward. For instance, pain not only has sensory qualities like vision and audition, but it also has motivating or drive aspects to it. A good example of this is the fact that we can readily identify which tooth is involved when we have a toothache because of the sensory qualities of the pain; we are also motivated to focus all of our attention on the toothache until it has been dealt with. In general, pain demands our attention until we are successful in relieving it.

In addition to having this motivational quality, pain differs from the other senses in another interesting way: The pain sense is not specialized for only one form of physical energy. Pain can be produced quite effectively by electrical, thermal, chemical, or mechanical stimulation, whereas the other senses respond best to a single form of energy. At one time it was thought that pain was not a separate sense modality but that it was the sensation that resulted from overstimulation of any of the other senses. This view of pain was readily accepted, because most people are aware from personal experience that very bright light, loud sounds, intense pressure, or extreme temperatures (either hot or cold) can all cause pain. However, more recent investigations have shown that pain is not simply the result of intense stimulation of the other sensory modalities. Pain is now recognized as a separate sense modality with its own receptors and pathways to the brain.

The receptors for pain are called *free nerve endings*. Free nerve endings are a primitive form of sensory receptor, and pain is actually a primitive sensory quality. It seems to be analyzed by the more primitive parts of the brain. Free nerve endings are referred to as primitive sensory cells in that they have not developed a specificity for a single form of physical energy as have the other sensory receptors of the body. Some responses to pain are so reflexive and automatic that they are actually controlled at the level of the spinal cord and do not require the participation of the brain. For example if we accidentally place our hand on a sharp object such as a tack, a spinal defensive reflex causes us to withdraw our hand without any thought processes being involved. Usually we have begun to withdraw the injured hand even before we are aware that we have injured it. The withdrawal response is actually well underway before the pain message even reaches the brain.

Free nerve endings, the receptors for pain, are found mostly in the skin. However, they also occur in the muscles, tendons, joints, connective tissue of the visceral organs, the eardrums, and the corneas of the eyes. The presence of free nerve endings makes a scratched cornea or a ruptured eardrum a highly painful experience.

Interestingly, the brain itself and many of the internal organs do not possess free nerve endings. This means that the brain, which receives pain messages from all other parts of the body, would itself be insensitive to being poked with a sharp object or to being subjected to hot or cold stimulation. Because the brain contains no pain receptors and is therefore insensitive to pain, some forms of brain surgery on human patients are actually performed with the patient awake and conscious. Only a local anesthetic is used to deaden pain sensitivity in the scalp, skull, and the protective covering of the brain known as the *dura*. The patient is also given a drug to promote relaxation. The reason for keeping the patient awake is that the surgeon can use the patient's verbal reports to help determine what part of the brain is being worked on. Surgery on certain internal organs of the body such as the gall bladder can also be performed under local anesthetic. If the overlying skin and connective tissue surrounding the organ are desensitized, cutting or cauterization of the structure can be done while the patient is awake.

The location of pain receptors over the surface of the human body has been studied on a number of occasions. This mapping of pain spots has been done with pin pricks, with thermal probes, by focusing a high intensity light bulb on a small patch of skin, and by a spark gap technique (where a spark is generated and made to jump from an electrode to a small spot on the skin surface). All of these methods have yielded similar results. The concentration of pain receptors is greatest along the midline axis of the body and decreases as we move outward toward the extremities. Thus, the abdomen contains many more free nerve endings than do the fingertips, and as a consequence, the pain sensitivity of the abdomen is approximately twenty times greater than the pain sensitivity of the same size spot on the fingertip. That portion of the body having the greatest pain sensitivity seems to be the cornea of the eye, being approximately thirty times more sensitive than the abdomen.

Two exceptions to the general rule that midline structures of the body are densely populated with free nerve endings are the mucosal linings of the cheeks, and the rear of the tongue. As a child I once had occasion to observe the "human pin cushion" in a carnival side show. This man claimed to be able to stick hat pins into any portion of his body without feeling any pain. On the evening in question he "just happened" to chose to stick them through his cheeks. I was suitably impressed when this man pushed two large hat pins through each of his cheeks and then opened his mouth so that his audience could see that indeed the pins had penetrated through his skin. Thirty years later I found out that the human pin cushion was making use of the anatomical fact that portions of the cheek have a relatively low concentration of free nerve endings, and that this was probably the only part of his body through which he stuck hat pins.

Regarding the relative lack of free nerve endings on the back of the tongue, the ability of some individuals to sip coffee or tea near the boiling point is dependent on this anatomical fact. There is a slight trick involved in drinking hot liquids without suffering pain. One must first take a sharp sip of air to cool the surface of the palate. Then, the hot liquid must be quickly moved to the relatively insensitive back of the tongue and swallowed fast before the temperature of the skin tissue becomes high enough that pain is experienced. It is important that the hot liquid not come into contact with the front part of the tongue. This portion of the tongue contains enough pain receptors that even the cooling sip of air is insufficient to eliminate the experience of pain.

It was mentioned earlier that pain has both sensory aspects and motivational aspects. These two aspects of pain can be dissociated from each other by a drastic surgical procedure known as a *prefrontal lobotomy*. The prefrontal lobotomy is an operation where the nerve fibers connecting the frontal lobes to the rest of the brain are severed. The usual result of such an operation is that the person so treated becomes calm, placid, and much less emotional. Because of these behavioral changes, in the 1940s and 1950s prefrontal lobotomies would sometimes be performed on mental patients who were highly emotional in an attempt to calm them down and make them more manageable. This surgical procedure is no longer used to calm mental patients, but it is sometimes used to provide relief for terminal cancer patients who are suffering intense pain and who have developed a tolerance for pain-reducing drugs. It has been noted that terminally ill pain victims stop complaining about their pain following a prefrontal lobotomy, and it was initially believed that the operation was able to eliminate pain perception. Later, it was discovered that the patients still perceived pain, but that they just did not care about it any more. The prefrontal lobotomy had eliminated the drive aspect of pain, but the sensory aspect was still present. The result was that the patients could still feel the pain, but they no longer complained about it.

It was mentioned that the brain itself possesses no pain receptors and is actually insensitive to pain. This seems somewhat strange in view of the fact that pain seems to be emanating from the brain when we experience a tension headache, a migraine headache, or the headache accompanying a hangover. Headache pain seems to be localized in the brain, but the actual source of the pain has been shown to be free nerve endings in the dura (the protective outer covering of the brain) and the blood vessels of the brain such as the meningeal artery. It may seem as though the brain is throbbing and pounding with each surge of our pulse, but this is not really what is happening. Raising the arterial blood pressure is known to intensify a headache, while lowering the arterial blood pressure is known to bring relief from a headache. Successful treatments for headache include rest and relaxation, quiet surroundings, and perhaps gentle massage; these procedures are known to lower the arterial blood pressure. In contrast to these procedures, engaging in sex, mowing the lawn, or jogging are examples of activities that should be avoided when one is in the grip of a bad hangover.

It was noted that the receptors for pain (free nerve endings) seem to be a primitive form of sensory receptor and that pain pathways project to more primitive parts of the brain. In higher animals such as human beings, cortical structures (the more intelligent and less reflexive parts of the brain) have developed the ability to exert some inhibitory control over our perception of pain. Thus we find that in people, as opposed to rats, such things as our expectations, past experiences, anxiety level, cultural background, and the meaning that we attach to a particular situation can all contribute to whether or not we will perceive a situation as painful. For example, a boxer may break his hand in the early rounds of a fight and not be aware of it until the fight is over; a soldier can be wounded in battle and not feel any pain until the danger is passed. In both cases, the individual's attention is directed elsewhere and the pain is not perceived. In our Western culture there is the general expectation that childbirth will be painful, and indeed most women in our society report that it is painful. In some non-Western societies, there is no expectation that pain will be associated with childbirth, and women from these societies do not describe it as a painful experience. The effects of one's level of anxiety on pain perception have been well documented. Receiving an injection in the doctor's office hurts more if we are tense and anxious than if we are relaxed and calm. Actually, the ability of morphine to reduce pain is not because morphine acts directly on pain centers in the brain, but because morphine lowers the anxiety level of the treated individual. When an individual suffering from chronic pain develops a tolerance to morphine, the drug is no longer effective in reducing pain.

Perhaps the most dramatic illustration of the control that higher mental processes can exert on pain perception is found in the phenomenon of suggestibility. It is well known that hypnosis, which is an extreme form of suggestibility, can increase a person's pain tolerance. However, less extreme forms of suggestibility can also reduce pain sensitivity. The importance of suggestibility in dealing with pain is so well known in the health professions that it is given a special name, the *placebo effect*. When a physician gives a "sugar pill" to a hypochondriac and tells him or her that the pill is a new miracle drug, and if the hypochondriac suddenly feels better, he or she is demonstrating the placebo effect. In mass emergencies such as large fires, health professionals administering on-the-spot treatment have been known, upon running out of morphine, to give burn victims injections of distilled water and tell them it was morphine. In such instances, it is not uncommon for 35 percent of the victims to experience a reduction in their pain because they think they have received morphine. This a dramatic demonstration of the placebo effect at work. It should be noted that there is a difference of opinion in the medical profession at this time regarding the use of the placebo effect. Some physicians feel that if they can provide relief to a patient by administering a placebo treatment then it is perfectly justified. Other physicians view placebo treatments as unethical because it involved deception of the patient. As is usually the case in such controversies, both arguments appear to have some merit.

Some nerve fibers have been identified that travel from the brain back to the peripheral parts of the body. Such pathways might be the means by which the higher parts of the brain are able to control pain perception in different regions of the body. However, it is clear that there is still a great deal about pain perception that is not understood at the present time.

One obvious example of our lack of understanding of pain perception is the phenomenon of *acupuncture*. Acupuncture is a method of reducing or eliminating pain through the insertion of thin needles into different parts of the body. Acupuncture anesthesia has been practiced in China for thousands of years; yet until recently, it had been dismissed by Western scientists as unworthy of their attention, being at best an Oriental version of the placebo effect. In the past few years, however, Western scientists have begun to pay serious attention to acupuncture anesthesia because there is now very strong evidence that it actually works. Teams of physicians from the United States, Britain, and other Western countries have traveled to China and observed for themselves major surgery being performed on people with acupuncture needles serving as the anesthetic. In one such operation, a man had part of his lung surgically removed, with a single needle inserted in the right biceps muscle and rotated for 10 to 15 seconds every minute serving as the only anesthetic. Another patient had a stomach ulcer removed, the anesthetic consisting of four acupuncture needles inserted in each ear and wired to a DC battery. In another instance, a thyroid operation was performed with needles in the wrist and the back of the neck providing the anesthetic.

In view of this sort of documented evidence, clearly the relevant question to ask is no longer "does acupuncture anesthesia work?" but rather "how does acupuncture anesthesia work?" Several possible answers to this question have been proposed. The oldest (and least acceptable to Western science) answer is the Yang and Yin theory of the ancient Chinese. In this theory, disharmony between Yang (the blood) and Yin (the spirit) produces pain. Insertion of the needles in one or more of the 365 acupuncture sites along the 12 meridians of the body, which are depicted in Figure 15, was supposed to bring Yang and Yin back into harmony and thus relieve pain. Up until recently, a more popular theory among Western scientists was that patients undergoing surgery with acupuncture anesthesia were probably under the influence of some form of hypnosis. However, several factors rule out the possibility that hypnosis is the answer to the effectiveness of acupuncture. First, observation of patients indicates that during surgery they are awake, alert, and not in a hypnotic trance. Some patients undergoing surgery

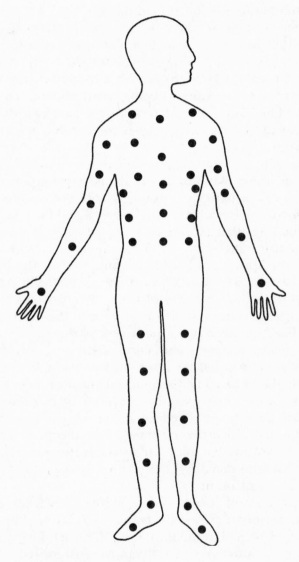

Figure 15. Acupuncture points along 6 of the 12 meridians in the human body.

with acupuncture needles providing anesthetic relief from pain have been observed to carry on a normal conversation during the surgical procedure. Also, acupuncture anesthesia has been used successfully with infants, which reduces the plausibility of the hypnosis theory. Finally, there are reports (and movies) of acupuncture anesthesia being used during surgery on animals. This usage would tend to completely rule out any form of suggestibility as the basis for the analgesic effects of acupuncture.

The explanation for the pain-blocking effects of acupuncture favored by most Western scientists is based upon the *gate-control theory* of pain first proposed by professors Patrick Wall and Ronald Melzack over ten years ago. The gate-control theory proposes that pain is experienced when transmission of pain impulses takes place from the site of injury in the body, through the spinal cord, to the brain. It is in the brain that pain awareness is registered. In order to reach the brain, pain messages from the periphery of the body must pass through a cluster of cells in the spinal cord known as the *substantia gelatinosa*. The substantia gelatinosa acts as the gate in the gate-control theory. When these nerve cells are activated, pain impulses are blocked at the level of the spinal cord and they do not reach the brain. The gate-control theory predicts that any procedure which increases the electrical activity in the substantia gelatinosa would reduce or abolish pain by increasing the inhibitory properties of these cells, thereby "closing the gate" on transmission of pain messages to the brain. If the brain is not stimulated by these pain impulses, then pain perception does not occur.

The gate-control theory is compatible with what is known about the sensory nerves of the body. Two classes of nerve fibers have been identified in the skin, large diameter, fast-conducting nerve fibers (called A-alpha fibers by anatomists) and small diameter, slower-conducting nerve fibers (called C fibers). The large fibers for the most part are known to receive input from touch, pressure, warmth, and cold receptors in the skin. The small fibers seem to be associated with free nerve endings in the skin. Large A-alpha fibers, when activated, are thought to increase the electrical activity in the substantia gelatinosa; the

smaller C fibers appear to decrease the activity in the substantia gelatinosa. The gate-control theory proposes that increased activity in the substantia gelatinosa should block pain transmission to the brain by "closing the gate." Most stimuli applied to the skin will excite both large nerve fibers and small nerve fibers. If more large fibers than small fibers are excited, the stimulus will be perceived as touch, pressure, warmth, or cold. If more small fibers than large fibers are stimulated, the sensation of pain will be experienced because the "gate" in the substantia gelatinosa will be opened and pain messages will travel to the brain. What is important in determining whether or not pain will be perceived is the ratio of large to small nerve fibers that are activated by a particular stimulus. The gate-control theory of pain predicts that anything increasing the level of activity in large nerve fibers should have the effect of reducing pain sensations. Indeed, this seems to be the case. Rubbing an insect bite takes away the sting; hot water bottles, ice packs, mustard plasters, massage, and whirlpool treatments are all effectively used to treat pain. All of these treatments are known to stimulate large A-alpha nerve fibers in the body.

Returning our attention to acupuncture, recall that the needles are not simply placed in the skin and left alone. The needles are vibrated, twirled, or have a DC current passed through them. The ancient Chinese practitioners sometimes burned herbs at the top of the needle, and presumably the heat was transferred down the shaft of the needle to temperature receptors in the skin. Thus, acupuncture needles could actually be stimulating large nerve fibers in the skin, and overcoming pain by countering the tendency of the small C fibers to open the "gate" in the substantia gelatinosa.

Remaining to be explained is how acupuncture needles could be reducing pain at sites on the body that are physically removed from the spot where the needle or needles are inserted. For example, how could a needle inserted in the right biceps muscle reduce pain during a thyroid operation? Here again professors Wall and Melzack have proposed an answer. It has been determined experimentally in cats and other animals that regions of the brainstem, when electrically stimulated, can produce a deep analgesic effect over large areas of the body. If acupuncture needles were inserted so they stimulated nerves traveling to these inhibitory regions of the brainstem, it would be possible to reduce pain perception in body parts at a distance from the location of the needles — because the needles would excite these inhibitory regions of the brainstem, and inhibitory fibers would then descend from the brainstem and produce analgesia in the appropriate regions of the body.

Neurological examination of patients suffering from certain diseases lends support to the gate-control theory of pain. Occasionally a degenerative disease of the nervous system attacks only small C fibers and leaves the large A-alpha fibers intact. Patients with such a condition show decreased pain sensitivity, as is predicted by the gate-control theory. On the other hand, following infection with herpes zoster virus, some individuals tend to perceive even a light touch as extremely painful. In such individuals the ratio of large to small nerve fibers has been reduced, and the resulting change in pain sensitivity is again in line with the prediction of the gate-control theory.

One obvious implication of the gate-control theory of pain is that if a chemical substance could be found that produces excitation in the substantia gelatinosa, the problem of pain would be solved. Unfortunately at the present time such a chemical substance has not been identified. The gate-control theory is currently our best guess as to why acupuncture can relieve pain. The fact that it is still called a *theory* is evidence that many questions remain to be answered about pain.

Pain Perception and Age

There is relatively little information available about changes in pain sensitivity that occur as a function of age. A further problem is seen in the fact that the existing information is somewhat contradictory. On the one hand, society sometimes jokes about the way that older people are supposed to complain about their aches and pains. The implication here is that older people may be more sensitive to pain than younger people. On the other hand, some physicians report that older people tend to show less distress upon receiving injections and that in some cases elderly people can actually undergo minor surgery in the absence of anesthesia, without experiencing severe pain. These physicians believe that older people do not feel pain as intensely as young people. Which view is correct? Do older people feel pain more intensely or less intensely than young people? The answer seems to be that both statements are true. The conflict arises when we fail to specify what kind of pain we are talking about. Pain can be either "bright" (superficial) pain of the type produced by a needle puncture or an incision of the skin or "dull" (deep) pain of the type associated with an aching joint or a strained muscle.

Recently, two experiments have been reported that distinguish between superficial pain and deep pain. The human subjects used in these experiments ranged in age from eighteen to ninety years. In one experiment, a sharp, pricking pain sensation was produced by focusing a projecting lamp beam through a condensing lens onto a spot of skin. The intensity of the lamp was increased until the subject reported a sensation of pain. In another experiment, pressure was applied to the Achilles tendon of the ankle by squeezing it between two rods. Tension was increased until the subject reported a pain sensation. In the first experiment, sensitivity for the pricking pain was seen to decrease with age. In the second experiment, tolerance for pressure on the Achilles tendon was seen to be greater in the young subjects than in the old subjects. So it appears that, with increasing age, tolerance for superficial pain increases but tolerance for deep pain decreases. The underlying physical reasons for these sensitivity changes are not known at this time.

Chapter 9

THE KINESTHETIC SENSE

CONSIDER the degree of motor coordination required in performing a precise act such as threading a needle or playing the child's game of pick-up-sticks. Obviously, the control of one's movements must be highly accurate. It is not sufficient to simply contract certain muscles at certain times. There must be a continuous monitoring of the action of the muscles as related to the desired behavioral outcome. The *kinesthetic sense* is the sense modality that allows us to be aware of and to monitor muscular control of limb and trunk movement.

The kinesthetic modality can be divided into the *muscle sense* and the *joint sense*. The receptors for the muscle sense are contained in the muscles of the body and also in the tendons that attach the muscles to the bones. The receptors for the joint sense are found in the joint capsules and in the ligaments that hold our bones together at the joints. The arrangement of muscles, bones, joints, ligaments, and tendons is shown in Figure 16.

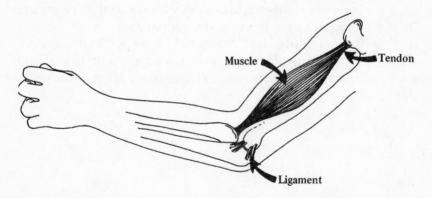

Figure 16. Diagram showing the relationship between muscles, tendons, bones, and ligaments.

96

Both the muscle sense receptors and the joint sense receptors are known as *mechanoreceptors,* because they respond to mechanical stimulation. Receptors in the muscles provide us with information about the muscles' state of contraction. Receptors in the tendons are able to detect and inform us when the tendons holding the muscle to bone are being stretched to the danger point by excessive contraction of the muscle. The receptors in the ligaments and joint capsules are sensitive to the angle of rotation of our joints. That is, these receptors provide us with information about the position of our limbs in space. The presence of the joint receptors enables us to be aware of the degree to which our elbows or knees are bent or straight, even with our eyes closed.

The feedback to the brain from kinesthetic receptors is what permits us to perform skilled motor activities. A large part of becoming proficient at sports such as golf or tennis is learning to use kinesthetic feedback from the muscles and joints to coordinate all of the body parts needed to strike the ball properly. It is not sufficient simply to read a book on how to play golf or tennis. One must practice the strokes over and over, thousands of times, in order to gain proficiency. What we are actually doing when we begin to acquire proficiency at some skilled act is learning "how it feels" when we do it right. There is no way to learn this by reading a book. We must learn to be sensitive to the kinesthetic feedback from our joints and muscles. These kinesthetic cues are not as obvious as the kinds of stimuli that we perceive with our eyes and ears. Thus we must make a concerted effort to learn to make use of feedback from our own movements that come from the muscle and joint senses.

Age Factors in Kinesthetic Sensitivity

It is well known that in old age there are predictable changes in motor performance. These changes are characterized by a decrease in muscular strength, decreased speed of muscular contraction, and a reduced coordination of fine movements. These changes are known to be due at least in part to deterioration of muscle fiber tissue. However, it is also likely that decreased feedback from kinesthetic receptors plays a role, especially in the finding of decreased coordination. If changes in feedback from kinesthetic receptors were occurring in the elderly, one might expect that some deficit in motor coordination would follow, because perception of movement of the body parts is a critical part of performing skilled activities.

Experimental evidence supports the idea that such kinesthetic feedback changes take place in the elderly. In one study, two groups of subjects were tested on their ability to detect slow passive rotation of their limbs. One group of subjects ranged in age from 17 to 35 years, and the other group ranged in age from 50 to 85 years. The subject's limbs were placed on a hinged platform. This platform could be slowly raised or lowered. In the absence of visual cues, the task of the subjects was to report whether a limb was being raised or lowered as soon as they detected a change in its position in space. The younger subjects were found to have greater sensitivity for detection of limb position. The older subjects, in addition to being less sensitive to limb position changes, showed greater variability in their judgments on repeated trials.

Clearly, changes in motor abilities occur with age. However, the fact that these changes occur is no reason for older people to give up participation in skilled activities such as golf or tennis. An intelligent approach would be for an older person to learn to depend more on strategy than on muscular strength, speed, and coordination. For example, shortening the backswing on a golf shot will reduce the distance that the ball will travel, but it will increase the accuracy of the shot. In the case of tennis, an older person must depend more on lobs and spins and learn to play a steady, error free, more strategic game, letting a younger opponent go for the big slam at the accompanying risk of committing an error. An acquaintance of mine seventy-four years of age uses this approach to tennis quite effectively, holding his own against opponents one-third his age.

Compensatory behaviors and strategies of the type mentioned in the case of golf and tennis undoubtedly exist for all kinds of skilled activities. The intelligent older person does not expect (for instance) to hit the ball as hard at sixty as he or she did at thirty. Rather, the older person should actively strive to find ways to substitute "brains for brawn" and continue participation in enjoyed physical activities.

Chapter 10

BRAIN MECHANISMS AND PERCEPTION

U P to this point we have been talking about physical changes in sensory systems that are related to the aging process and how these changes affect basic sensations. In the present chapter, we will talk about perception, rather than sensation. What, then, is the distinction between sensation and perception? Different people answer this question in different ways. For our purposes, a sensation is said to occur when physical energy at a detectable intensity impinges on the receptors of one of our sensory systems. Perception, on the other hand, refers to the way that we interpret sensory stimulation, to the meaning or significance that sensory stimuli have for us. For example, the red, white, and blue colors and patterns that stimulate our visual system when the American flag is carried by in a parade results in visual sensations; but the way the brain interprets this sensation, the feeling of national pride or patriotism that the sight of the flag is able to elicit in us, is an example of a perception. That is, the flag has come to acquire meaning for us, and the meaning of an object defines our perception of the object. Someone who has never seen the flag before would attach no special significance to this piece of cloth with red, white, and blue markings on it.

A perception, then, is more complicated than a sensation. Sensation is determined by the state of our sensory receptors, but perception is determined by such higher order processes as learning, past experience, expectations, motivation, emotional state, and our personality characteristics. Perception is influenced by the higher centers of the brain that play a role in all of the above, especially the cerebral cortex. The cerebral cortex is critical for all of our higher mental processes, including perception. To the extent that the aging process produces changes in the cerebral cortex of the brain, one should expect that aging will have an affect on the way we perceive the world.

In fact there is evidence that the aging process does alter our perception of the world. Let us first discuss some of this evidence, and then try to relate it to known changes in the brains of the elderly. One area of perception in which experimental work has been done with the aged deals with the perception of temporal sequences of stimuli. Electrical house current (at least in the United States) is 110 volt, 60 cycle per second alternating current. This means that our lights are actually flickering at a rate of 60 flickers per second. This rate of flicker is so fast that the human visual system cannot follow it, and instead of a flicker, we perceive the lights as a steady level of brightness. A similar effect is encountered when we go to the movies. What is appearing on the screen is a series of single frames of film that are being presented at such a rapid rate that we perceive continuous movement rather than a sequence of individual pictures.

Let us return our attention to 60 cycle house current. If we were to slowly reduce the rate of flicker of a light from its normal 60 cycle per second condition, we would find that the eye of a young adult human continues to perceive a constant, fused light down to a rate of around 41 flickers per second. Below this level, the flickering characteristic of the light stimulus is perceived. The value at which a flickering light is perceived as being continuous, around 41 flickers per second in a young adult, is referred to as the *critical flicker frequency* or CFF. By age 60, the CFF has dropped from 41 to around 33 flickers per second. It appears that the elderly nervous system is less able to process rapid, successive visual inputs than is the young nervous system. As has already been noted, changes in the eyeball itself such as reduced peripheral vision, decrease in pupil size, and discoloration of the lens could possibly produce a reduction in CFF under some conditions. However, even when a bright white light is shined directly into the pupil, a drop of CFF is found in the elderly. This suggests that changes in the brain, not simply changes in the eyeball, are contributing to the lower CFF in the aged.

An auditory phenomenon has been reported that is similar in some ways to the visual CFF data. A train of clicks, if presented at a rapid enough rate, will fuse into a steady sound.

Trains of clicks have been found to fuse into a steady sound at a lower rate for elderly listeners than for young listeners; at rates below the fusion level, a given rate of click presentation is perceived differently by young and old listeners. For a given burst of clicks, older persons perceive the number of clicks contained in the burst as being fewer than the number of clicks reported by young listeners. As in the case of visual CFF, changes in information processing speed in the brain rather than peripheral factors such as presbycusis seem to be the basis for this change in click-rate perception. In support of this idea, we have found that partial destruction of the temporal lobe in the cat brain reduces the animal's ability to perceive the rate of presentation of trains of clicks even though the animal's sensitivity to single clicks or tone pulses remains unchanged.

A direct test has been made of the suggestion that young persons and older persons perceive temporal properties of the environment differently. Two groups of subjects, one group having a mean age of twenty-four and the other having a mean age of sixty-seven, were tested on their ability to estimate lengths of time ranging from 30 to 300 seconds. Compared to the younger group, the older subjects consistently underestimated these periods of time. This finding is in complete agreement with the reports of lower CFF and click-fusion rates in the elderly. If information processing in the aged nervous system is taking place at a slower rate, a given interval of time would be perceived as passing faster for an old person as compared with a young person. In a way, the phenomenon is analogous to speeding up the film in a motion picture projector. The perception of small details is reduced, and the events depicted in the film appear to take place at a faster rate. In the case of comparing time estimation in a young person and an older person, events in the world take place at their usual speed; because of a slower information processing rate, they seem to be occurring faster to the older perceiver. Thus, when asked to estimate an interval of time, the older group underestimates it because they perceive events as occurring faster in time than is actually the case.

For human beings, of considerably more importance than the

ability to detect flickering lights, trains of clicks, or even to estimate the passage of time is the ability to perceive speech. Speech, being composed of successively occurring sounds, might be expected to show perceptual changes with age just as is known to happen with trains of clicks. Indeed, this expectation is confirmed. Evidence suggests that in elderly people there is a decrease in speech perception (hearing what was said) as well as in speech comprehension (understanding what was said) that is too great to be accounted for by peripheral factors such as presbycusis. This deficit seems to be related to a change in the speed of information processing in the brain. Reduced speech comprehension in the elderly is especially serious in situations where the environment contains background noise or other forms of distraction. For example, the "cocktail party" phenomenon is less apparent in the elderly than in young adults. The cocktail party phenomenon refers to the remarkable ability that people have of "tuning out" extraneous sounds and attending to one auditory input at a time. This is of course what one must do at a cocktail party, where the entire room is a buzzing jumble of human voices and laughter, yet we possess the ability to ignore most of this auditory input and attend only to the voice of the individual who is speaking to us. The elderly have more difficulty with speech comprehension in a cocktail party situation because of the background noise.

A deficit in speech comprehension is characteristic of the aged, probably resulting from reduced efficiency of information transmission in the nervous system. The additional deficit experienced in a cocktail party situation probably results from a reduction in *vigilance,* which has also been noted in the elderly. Vigilance refers to the ability to fix one's attention on one aspect of the environment and maintain one's attention even in the presence of distracting stimuli. A procedure known as the Mackworth Clock Test is used to test vigilance in the laboratory situation. The Mackworth Clock Test has indicated that vigilance declines with age. Subjects of various ages were asked to watch a moving hand as it swept around a clock face. The hand was programmed to stop its movement for a brief time at irregular intervals. The job of the subject was to detect these occasions when the hand stopped moving and to signal the fact that they had detected the stop by pressing a button. Vigilance behavior as measured by the Mackworth Clock Test has been shown to fall off after age sixty. A decline in vigilance would have implications for speech perception and comprehension, especially in situations involving background noise.

The kinds of perceptual deficits we have been discussing up to now are probably the result of general changes that occur in all parts of the brain. We will describe some of these general changes shortly. It is also the case that speech perception and comprehension can be affected by damage to specific parts of the brain known as speech areas. The human brain is unique among all animal brains in that certain important functions come to be controlled by a single hemisphere rather than being bilaterally represented. Speech is an example of such an important function. The left hemisphere of the brain in most right-handed people contains the speech centers. While some left-handed people have their speech centers in the right hemisphere, many have them in the left hemisphere; thus, handedness is not a certain method for determining which hemisphere of the brain controls a person's speech.

The term *aphasia* is used to refer to conditions whereby damage to the speech areas of the brain results in disruption of the associative skills of language. There are two main categories of aphasia. *Expressive aphasia* denotes a condition where the patient knows what he or she wants to say but is unable to say it. People with expressive aphasia can have problems with any or all of the following: (1) articulation — inability to produce speech sounds, (2) word fluency — may be able to produce sounds and perhaps individual words but cannot put them together to express coherent thoughts, (3) word finding — an inability to name common objects, action words, colors, etc. Expressive aphasia is associated with damage to a part of the brain known as *Broca's area*. Broca's area is quite close to the motor areas of the brain, and thus it is not surprising that damage to Broca's area produces an expressive deficit.

Of more direct relevance to our discussion of perceptual deficits is the second category of aphasia, *receptive aphasia*. Here,

the problem is not one of word fluency but rather one of understanding the speech of others. Someone with receptive aphasia
can still hear sounds, but speech loses its special communica-
tive significance. Affected individuals can no longer recognize
words as being meaningful. The part of the brain involved in
receptive aphasia is called *Wernicke's area*. Wernicke's area is
located near that part of the cerebral cortex responsible for
auditory sensitivity. Both Broca's area and Wernicke's area are
located in the left cerebral hemisphere in most right-handed
people. These two speech areas are depicted in Figure 17. It is
of considerable interest that some people suffering from Wernicke's aphasia can still communicate by reading and writing.
This means that speech, reading, and writing are controlled by
different regions of the brain.

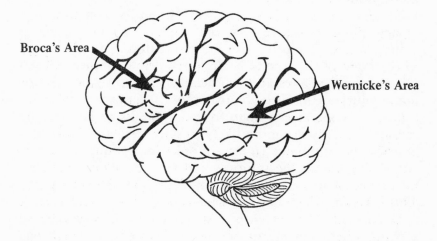

Figure 17. Lateral view of left hemisphere of human brain, showing location
of the speech areas.

Of the two categories of aphasia, the prognosis for recovery is
better for expressive than it is for receptive. One relatively new
form of therapy for both types of aphasia victims that is generating a lot of interest is called *melodic intonation therapy* or
MIT. MIT is based upon the idea that while speech is generally
under the control of the left hemisphere of the brain, musical

ability as well as an undeveloped potential for the use of language reside in the right hemisphere. Thus it is felt that aphasia victims may make progress toward recovery of language behavior if therapy takes the form of having the victims listen to, and sing, words and sentences. The use of melody seems to bring about an involvement of the undamaged, musically inclined right hemisphere, making use of its undeveloped language potential in this manner. In one test of melodic intonation therapy, two groups of aphasia victims were compared on their degree of progress over a six-month period. One group of patients received traditional forms of therapy, while the other group received MIT. Six of the eight patients in the MIT group showed significant recovery of language behavior, a more favorable outcome than was realized in the group undergoing traditional therapy.

Of course, aphasia is a more serious and less common form of perceptual deficit than is seen solely as a consequence of aging. Aphasia typically does not result from general changes in the brain of the type to be discussed below. Rather, aphasia usually occurs as a result of left hemispheric stroke, penetrating brain injury, or localized brain tumor. Aphasia is much more common in the elderly than in young adults or children because the elderly are more likely to suffer cerebrovascular disorders or brain tumors. In fact, in order for a young child to be an aphasia victim the injury would have to involve both hemispheres of the brain rather than just the left hemisphere. This is because the process by which speech and language come to be controlled by the left hemisphere takes time to develop. If a child suffers damage to one brain hemisphere, speech will simply come to reside in the undamaged hemisphere. However, in an adult, specialization (usually) of the left hemisphere has already occurred, and damage to this hemisphere will result in aphasia. As is probably obvious from this discussion, right-handed adults who suffer stroke damage or penetrating injury to the right hemisphere do not develop aphasia.

Having identified some forms of perceptual changes occurring in the elderly, let us now describe some age-related changes in the brain that may be the basis for the perceptual changes. One obvious difference between the brain of a young person and the brain of an elderly person is seen in the absolute number of brain cells that each possesses. A human infant is born with all the brain cells (called *neurons*) that he or she will ever have. Neurons have finite life span, and they begin to die in childhood and continue to die off for the rest of our lives. Another unfortunate property of neurons is that they do not regenerate and replace themselves as do cells in other parts of the body. When a neuron dies it is lost forever. The cerebral cortex of the human brain starts out with around 10 billion neurons, so we can easily afford to lose some of them with no resulting intellectual impairment. However, in old age the number of lost neurons may become so great that deficits in cognitive capacity begin to occur. In extreme cases, the loss of brain cells in the elderly reaches such an extent that the condition known as *senility* occurs. It has been estimated that a senile individual may be losing as many as 100,000 brain cells *per day*. Senility is known to affect reasoning, problem solving, and short-term memory. Not surprisingly, senility also affects perception in a variety of ways. In addition to a decrease in the absolute number of cells in the brain, the aging process has been associated with a reduction in the speed with which the remaining neurons conduct information. Decreased conduction speed in the brain could slow down the rate with which information is processed in the elderly nervous system. With regard to CFF, click fusion, and speech comprehension, the elderly nervous system may be less able to separately process each flash, click, or speech sound; as a result, fusion is perceived at a lower repetition rate and confusion of successive speech sounds takes place.

Certain changes in the blood supply to the brain are also known to be more common in the elderly. These vascular changes are of importance because they can bring about a serious reduction in the oxygen supply to the brain. Reduced oxygen to the brain (called *cerebral anoxia*) is known to impair not only perceptual abilities but intellectual capacities in general. In addition, cerebral anoxia hastens the rate at which brain cells die. The two most common vascular changes noted in the elderly are arteriosclerosis, or hardening of the arteries, and atherosclerosis, a buildup of fatty deposits in the walls of the blood vessels. Both of these conditions reduce blood flow, thereby reducing the oxygen supply to the brain.

Cerebral vascular accident (CVA), more commonly known as stroke, is also distressingly common in the elderly. Between 2 and 2.5 million Americans have suffered CVA. CVA occurs when (1) a clot is formed in a cerebral artery, (2) an artery ruptures, or (3) an artery is compressed by a skull fracture or a tumor. When CVA is caused by a stationary clot, the condition is referred to as a *thrombosis*. A moving clot, on the other hand, is called an *embolism*. The degree of impairment following CVA depends upon a number of factors including such things as which brain hemisphere is involved, the amount and location of tissue damage, the age of the individual at the time of injury, and the individual's motivation to recover.

Biochemical Changes in the Brain

As was noted earlier, conduction of information in the nervous system is an electrochemical process. The biochemical agents necessary for nerve conduction are called *transmitter substances*. One important transmitter substance that has been identified in the brains of both human beings and lower vertebrates is *dopamine*. Dopamine has been shown to be necessary for normal functioning of those parts of the brain that control temperature regulation, eating and drinking, sexual behavior, postural adjustment, and initiation of movement, and possibly some aspects of vision. It is worth mentioning that these behaviors are frequently seen to undergo some degree of deficit in the elderly. Thus it would not be surprising to find some change in dopamine levels in the brains of older people as compared to the levels in the brains of young adults.

Indeed, reduced levels of dopamine have been found in the brains of patients suffering from Parkinson's disease, and Parkinsonism is a condition found primarily in the elderly. Parkinson's disease is characterized by a number of sensorimotor deficiencies including (1) difficulty in initiating movements such as walking or rising from a chair; (2) difficulty in maintaining balance or showing normal postural adjustment in response to a shifting center of gravity; (3) tremor in the upper extremities and sometimes in the lower. While the majority of Parkinsonian patients are in the sixties and seventies, some early symptoms may be discovered in patients in their fifties. These early symptoms are seen to become progressively more severe, presumably as the depletion of dopamine in the patient's brain becomes progressively greater.

The relationship between dopamine depletion in the brain and Parkinson's disease is well established. Many patients have had their symptoms reduced or abolished by taking a drug called *l-dopa*. When taken orally, l-dopa travels to the brain, where it is converted into dopamine. The proper dosage of l-dopa must be determined individually for each Parkinsonian patient. Whereas dopamine depletion produces a general lack of responsiveness to the environment, too high a dosage of l-dopa can produce the opposite effect. The patients may become hyperactive, and in some instances suffer from hallucinations and symptoms of schizophrenia, a severe psychotic disorder. When the dosage of l-dopa is reduced, these undesirable side effects quickly disappear. Because of this apparent relationship between dopamine, l-dopa, Parkinson's disease, and schizophrenia, some researchers have proposed that Parkinsonism and schizophrenia are two extreme end-points on a continuum of dopamine activity in the brain. Dopamine depletion seems to result in Parkinsonism, while a dopamine excess may produce schizophrenic symptoms. In support of this idea are reports in the clinical literature that drugs such as Thorazine®, which are useful in treating schizophrenic symptoms, are known to block the efficiency of the dopamine system in the brain. Of further interest in this regard is the observation that too large a dose of Thorazine administered to a schizophrenic patient can produce the symptoms of Parkinson's disease. Apparently the way in which we respond to our environment is highly dependent upon the state of our brain dopamine system.

There is some speculation that dopamine reduction in the brain may occur as a natural consequence of the aging process.

Many elderly persons who are not actually Parkinsonian patients show some degree of tremor in their upper extremities. Perhaps this is indicative of a low level of dopamine depletion; possibly if we all lived long enough we would all experience sufficient dopamine depletion to end up with Parkinson's disease. The mechanism that would cause depletion of dopamine to take place faster in some people than others is not known at this time, although some researchers speculate that a hereditary factor may be involved.

Brain dopamine levels have not been measured in normal (asymptomatic) elderly humans, however, they have been measured in normal elderly rodents. Old mice have been shown to have 25 percent less dopamine in certain parts of their brains when compared to young mice. Also, it is possible to experimentally deplete the brain dopamine in a young adult rat and essentially produce a condition that resembles Parkinson's disease in the the animal. Dopamine-depleted rats show a general lack of responsiveness to their environment. They show an inability to initiate movement, difficulty with postural adjustment, and tremor. "Parkinsonian" rats show tremor in their tails rather than in the upper extremities. These symptoms can be reduced or abolished by giving the rats l-dopa, just as with humans. These findings with lower animals lead one to suspect that, if one were to measure brain dopamine levels in non-Parkinsonian elderly humans, one would find some degree of dopamine depletion, although not as great a depletion as is present in Parkinsonian patients.

Some rather exciting recent findings with laboratory rats suggest that it may be possible to protect an animal against dopamine depletion in old age. In normal rats, the dopamine-producing system in the brain has been shown to be activated during emotional (either pleasant or unpleasant) episodes, during periods of stress such as having their tails pinched, and during periods of vigorous activity. Rats that were subjected to repeated stress treatments which increased their dopamine production showed higher dopamine levels for a period of time that lasted longer than the duration of the stress treatment. The implication is that the dopamine-producing system of the brain may behave in a manner analogous to a muscle. That is, the more it is exercised, and the more vigorously it is exercised, the stronger and more efficient it becomes. If the dopamine system of the brain does in fact respond to frequent activation in a manner similar to the way a muscle develops with repetitive use, one might expect that old people who remain physically active and maintain a life-style that includes a variety of challenging, interesting, and occasionally stress-producing activities would be less likely to fall prey to the consequences of dopamine depletion. Of course, the converse of this suggestion is that an old person who gives up physical activity and adopts a sedentary, monotonous, uninteresting life style may be more likely to show signs of age-related dopamine depletion.

While no conclusive data exist at this time to support these speculations, the incidental observations of several physicians certainly point to their validity. That is, some physicians have noted that elderly people who are physically active, or who are still employed in a challenging occupation, show less tremor than elderly people who are retired and spend their time doing little or nothing. Obviously, at this time we are dealing with a situation resembling the old "which came first, the chicken or the egg" puzzle. Do some old people show less tremor because they are more active, or are they more active because they have less tremor? As was noted above, the answer to this question is not known with certainty at this time. However, it is clear that remaining physically active in one's later years cannot hurt, and it may turn out to be of immense benefit.

Chapter 11

ATTITUDE TOWARD SENSORY
DEFICIENCIES

AFTER reading the material in the pre-
ceeding chapters, one might be left with a distinctly pessimistic
feeling about what the aging process has done, is doing, or will
do to our sensory capacities. Indeed, at first glance such a pessimistic attitude seems warranted. In general, our sensory systems are going to experience a decline in old age. However, the
underlying message in these chapters is actually one that
should elicit in us a note of optimism. This message is that *we
are not totally and completely at the mercy of some unalterable
process that is going to impair all our senses.* While some
decline is inevitable, we have at our disposal the ability to
influence the amount and extent to which our senses will undergo age-related deterioration. We also have sufficient information to deal intelligently with those aspects of sensory
deterioration that are beyond our control.

We have seen that nutritional factors, vascular changes, general health, level of physical activity, environmental factors,
smoking, and prolonged use of certain drugs and antibiotics
can all play a part in contributing to sensory deficits in the
aged. All of these factors are under our control to some extent.
The present chapter will include suggestions for insuring that
we maximize our control over these factors.

Environmental Factors

Recall from the chapter on hearing that short-term exposure
to a noisy environment is known to produce a temporary decrease in auditory sensitivity, while prolonged exposure to such
an environment will almost certainly lead to a permanent
hearing loss. The message in this case is quite clear. Avoid loud
noises whenever possible. If you must work in a noisy occupa-

112

tion, wear ear plugs. If you hunt or trap shoot, wear protective ear coverings. Do not rent or buy a house near an airport or other noisy area. Experiments have shown that guinea pigs exposed to the noise of jet aircraft experience degenerative changes in the auditory hair cells. It is even a good idea to be sure that the muffler on your power lawn mower is working properly, as this level of noise can desensitize the auditory system. While it is less likely to be of concern to elderly listeners, prolonged exposure to high intensities of rock music can produce permanent hearing loss.

In the case of the visual modality, most people are aware of the potentially harmful consequences of looking directly at the sun, even during a solar eclipse. We would extend this caution and recommend that sunglasses be worn in bright sunlight even if you do not look toward the sun.

There are also some less obvious aspects of the environment that can influence our perceptual abilities. Apparently, the human organism requires a varied, constantly changing, interesting pattern of sensory inputs in order for our perceptual processes to remain intact. Too monotonous a sensory environment can dull or distort our perceptions, and in some instances actually produce hallucinations. Expressions such as going "stir crazy," having "cabin fever," or suffering from "kayak disease" give evidence to the fact that profound changes can occur in people who are confined for extended periods of time in a restricted sensory environment. The effectiveness of the "brain washing" technique used by the Chinese Communists during the Korean War is thought to be due to the denial of sensory stimulation to the victims.

The effects of a more extreme form of monotonous sensory environment have been studied in the laboratory under the name *sensory deprivation*. In a typical sensory deprivation experiment, human subjects are paid by the hour or day to lie on a cot in a sound-shielded room. The subjects wear translucent goggles, ear muffs, and cardboard tubes around their arms and legs to keep tactile and kinesthetic sensations from limb movements to a minimum. Subjects are asked to serve in the experiment for two or three days and are given two or three hours out of the sensory deprivation condition each day during which time they are fed, toileted, and given a variety of perceptual tests. When tested with the goggles removed after forty-eight hours of deprivation, virtually all subjects show significant perceptual distortions. Stationary objects in the visual field seem to be moving. The walls of the room appear to move in and out. Straight surfaces seem to be curved. The ability to estimate the size of objects at a distance is noticeably impaired. Subjects also report difficulty in concentrating and in thinking coherently. Some subjects find it difficult to talk, even hours after being removed from the deprivation situation. Performance on the Macworth Clock Test and other measures of vigilance falls off dramatically. Occasionally, subjects experience visual, auditory, and tactile hallucinations. Less intense effects have been reported in situations where the degree of sensory deprivation is less severe. For instance, subjects placed in an iron lung report perceptual distortion and disruption of thought processes. This is presumably due to the monotonous sound of the motor and the restriction of limb movement as well as the impoverishment of the visual environment.

The adverse effects of sensory deprivation are not restricted to human beings. Rats and mice that have been subjected to sensory deprivation show a variety of behavioral effects such as agitation, nervous twitches, and in some cases, convulsions. It appears that many different animals have a need for a varied diet of sensory experiences.

Granted, most people outside of the laboratory never experience the degree of sensory deprivation imposed in these kinds of experiments. However, studies show that radar operators, astronauts, submarine crews, and other individuals confined to a small area with a restricted range of sensory inputs tend to experience milder versions of the effects seen in the sensory deprivation experiments. This situation is of special importance for the elderly, because many older persons live in a self-imposed state of sensory deprivation. The elderly man or woman who has few if any friends, who withdraws from contact with the outside world, and who spends hours sitting in a small, quiet room, is probably doing some harm to his or her perceptual and cognitive abilities. The elderly individual who maintains an active interest in outside activities, and who is exposed to a varied sensory environment, is less likely to experience perceptual distortions of the variety described above.

Nutrition

Proper nutrition is important for people at any age. Normal functioning of the body can only occur when there is adequate material in the diet to fuel the biochemical processes that underlie our behavior. The nutritional needs of the elderly include the same quantities of protein, vitamins, and minerals as required by young adults. However, the total intake of calories of an older person should be reduced to compensate for lower basal metobolic rate and, in most cases, a reduced level of physical activity. Nutritional problems sometimes occur because interest in eating tends to decrease in the elderly. An older person who is eating alone may not feel like taking the trouble to prepare adequately balanced meals for just him- or herself. Also, the decrease in taste sensitivity that accompanies the aging process may take some of the enjoyment out of eating, with the result that mealtime loses much of its importance. With the added economic problems that sometimes beset the elderly, eating adequate meals can require budgeting, good planning, and careful preparation. Many older people come to the conclusion that proper eating habits are not worth the trouble. It is my contention that adequate nutrition is most certainly worth the added effort when one recognizes that not only our perceptual abilities but our general well-being is at stake. Recall that a deficiency in vitamin A can reduce visual sensitivity, especially in dim light, in a person of any age. With the unavoidable changes in visual sensitivity that old age produces anyway, it is unreasonable and unintelligent to let a vitamin deficiency add to the problem. Some cases of night blindness have shown remarkable improvement when vitamin A is added to the diet of the affected individual.

The vascular changes most frequently found in the brains of senile people, arteriosclerosis and atherosclerosis, are especially pronounced in older persons with poor nutritional habits. A diet high in fat content and cholesterol, for example, is likely to be associated with atherosclerosis. In addition to being an important factor in the rate at which brain cells die off by contributing to cerebral anoxia, such a diet would increase the potentially harmful (to vision) changes in the choroid coat of the retina and in the ciliary muscles that control accommodation of the lens. It is worth emphasizing again that good nutrition is critical for the overall well-being of the older person. We have no control over the rate at which our skin wrinkles or our hair turns gray, but we do have control over what we consume or do not consume at mealtimes.

It should be noted in this regard that prolonged overuse of alcohol has definitely been shown to have harmful consequences for adults at any age. Part of the debilitating effects of alcohol stems from the fact that heavy drinkers are more likely to have poor eating habits, thereby compounding the problem. The consequences of alcoholism are well known and will not be discussed here. Medical opinion is divided concerning the individual who regularly drinks moderate amounts of alcohol. Many doctors have been known to recommend that an older person have a glass of wine at mealtime, or have a drink at the end of the day to help them relax or to improve their circulation. On the other hand, some doctors now believe that even a single drink of alcohol increases the probability that some cells in the brain will die. Recent laboratory evidence has led some physicians to accept the so-called "sludging" hypothesis regarding alcohol. The sludging hypothesis proposes that even a single drink of alcohol tends to cause red blood cells to cluster together in the bloodstream. These clusters of cells can still readily pass through the arteries of the body and the brain, but the hypothesis states that this "sludge" may produce small blockages in the tiny branches of the arteries called *arterioles* that carry oxygen to the brain cells in the deeper layers of the cerebral cortex. Such blockage can hasten the death of these brain cells due to cerebral anoxia. The results of one reported laboratory test suggest that sludging was present in blood samples drawn from young adult volunteers who had taken a single drink of alcohol. As was mentioned above, medical opinion is still mixed regarding the moderate use of alcohol. Some physicians feel that the beneficial effects of a drink or two outweigh the possible harm (if any) that may result from sludging. One may rationalize away indulgence in alcohol by using logic such as "there are more old drunks than old doctors, so drinking can't be that bad for you." But the available evidence to date indicates that if you choose to drink alcohol, moderation should be your guideline.

General Health

Of course, general health is intimately related to proper nutrition, but there are some other aspects of general health that are deserving of special mention. It goes without saying that everyone wishes for good health. Life becomes more worth living when one is in good physical condition. Over and above this "quality of life" factor, there are some important implications that poor health has for our sensory systems.

People who are chronically ill tend to require more diagnostic x rays than healthy individuals. Thus it is the case that the elderly, who have a disproportionately greater number of illnesses than young adults, receive more x rays than do young people. X rays in sufficient quantities are known to be harmful to the sex cells of the individual. This is why health professionals drape a lead-lined apron across the lap of a patient who is having an x ray taken, and the x-ray technician stands behind a shield when the x-ray machine is being used. The danger to the sex cells in an older female who is passed the reproductive age is not critical, nor is the danger to the sex cells of an elderly male who is either sexually inactive or who only has sexual relations with a postmenopausal female. Often overlooked is that x rays can also be harmful to cells in the body in addition to the sex cells. It will be recalled from previous chapters that both taste and smell sensitivity can be adversely affected by exposure to x rays. In the elderly, these two senses appear to experience an unavoidable decline in sensitivity anyway. One should not hasten to contribute to this process by submitting to unnecessary x rays. In this era of medical malpractice suits, many physicians routinely take x rays even when there is no obvious reason for doing so. They are reluctant to give the appearance of negligence. In the same vein, many patients are reluctant to speak up and ask if the x rays are really necessary. One should of course follow a physician's advice, but there is no harm in making certain that one is not being exposed to unnecessary x rays, even if Medicare is paying the bill.

Another important benefit of maintaining good health is that it eliminates the need for someone to take antibiotics. Antibiotics are clearly a boon and represent a major breakthrough in the field of health care. However, as was mentioned in our discussion of hearing, some antibiotics have ototoxic side-effects. That is, some antibiotics in sufficient quantities can damage sensory hair cells and can produce hearing loss or possibly vestibular dysfunction. Streptomycin was mentioned in this regard. Other mycin drugs which can have ototoxic side effects are gentamycin and kanamycin. Diuretics such as ethacrynic acid and furosemide can also produce hair cell deterioration. Less well known is the fact that in, large enough dosages, even a common drug like aspirin can impair normal hearing. Fortunately, the decrease in hearing sensitivity associated with aspirin is usually reversible when the drug is discontinued. This is not always true with other ototoxic substances. Some cases of drug-induced hearing loss have been shown to involve a permanent impairment. Any time a drug produces a ringing in the ears (tinnitus), the affected individual should be alterted to the potentially serious consequences for hearing sensitivity and possibly arrange for an audiometric examination.

Obviously, conditions of ill health occur from time to time when antibiotics or diuretics are necessary to promote recovery. One should do whatever is required to treat such illnesses as rapidly as possible so that drug administration can be kept to a minimum.

Physical Activity

The term "physical activity" calls to mind such behaviors as walking, jogging, bicycling, bowling, and playing golf, tennis, or other racquet sports such as paddle ball, racquet ball, or squash. While these kinds of activities are in fact the major focus of this section, physical activity can also refer to a hobby, participation in a club or organization, a part-time or full-time job, playing a musical instrument, or continuing one's formal education. Medical opinion supports the belief that participation in any of the above activities is beneficial not just for an older person, but for any adult. Children usually experience such joy in being physically active that they do not have to be "sold" on its virtues.

Let us concentrate on the value of physical activity for the older individual. Apart from the better appetite, improved condition of the circulatory system, and superior muscle tone present in older people who are physically active, participation in physical activities broadens one's circle of acquaintances and helps to provide varied sensory stimulation. One can also experience a feeling of pride in accomplishment as one's skill and endurance increases and one's waistline decreases. Old muscles benefit from exercise just as young ones do.

It seems appropriate here to reemphasize two critical points mentioned earlier about the value of physical activity. First, it was noted that physically active older people seem to be less affected by senile osteoporosis, the condition where the bones become porous and brittle. Second, it was speculated that high levels of physical activity may retard the depletion of dopamine in the brain, a condition thought by some researchers to be a common consequence of the aging process. These two factors alone should cause someone to reconsider if they have chosen to exclude physical activity from their lives. There are people in their seventies and eighties who regularly play golf and/or tennis and who take great pleasure in their participation in these activities, in addition to the fact that they are probably prolonging their lives, retarding senility, and (of course) preserving their sensory capacities.

What about the elderly person who is unable for medical reasons to engage in regular physical activity? In this situation it is suggested that participation in a hobby, membership in a club, getting a part-time job, or perhaps going back to college can go a long way toward providing the intellectual stimulation, the rewards, and the feelings of worth and accomplishment needed by both young and old alike.

More and more older people are returning to college (or starting college for the first time) under special programs for senior citizens. The University of Pittsburgh has instituted a policy whereby tuition is waived for retired persons who wish to audit certain undergraduate courses. In the past two years I have become acquainted with five people who have participated in this program when they attended my Introduction to Psychology class. One man's story is worth sharing because it makes a number of important points. Mr. X was seventy-three years old at the beginning of the term, and he visited me in my office to ask if I minded his presence in the class. I indicated that I was glad to have him in class, although he still had doubts about going to college at his age. Our society values youth, vigor, and physical attractiveness. Whether we are willing to admit it or not, society has a negative attitude toward the elderly, and the elderly come to share this negative attitude toward the elderly. As a result, Mr. X felt that "these young kids," as he referred to the rest of the class, were smarter and more academically inclined than he, and that he was probably doing something wrong by taking up a space in the class.

In spite of his doubts, Mr. X began to attend class regularly, although he always sat in a corner of the room and tried to remain as inconspicuous as possible by never contributing during class discussions. Occasionally he would talk with me after class and relate some personal experience he had had that was a perfect example of some point under discussion in class. Mr. X, it seems, had at various times in his life been a bartender, a soldier, a factory worker, a taxi cab driver, and finally a manufacturer's representative, a position he had held until company policy forced him to retire at age 65. His life experiences had been wide and varied. One day, after two hours of conversation, I convinced Mr. X that I found his life experiences fascinating (which was true) and that I was sure his classmates would benefit by hearing about some of them. To make a long story short, Mr. X began to contribute some of his experiences in class discussions. Sometimes his contributions were insightful, sometimes they provoked class discussion, sometimes they generated friendly arguments between Mr. X and some other member or members of the class. Mr. X began to interact with his classmates outside of class. He could regularly be seen with other students at the campus coffee shop. As he continued to gain confidence in himself (it had apparently been a shock and a blow to the ego to be told at age 65 that his company did not want him any more) it became clear that Mr. X had an excellent mind and an excellent sense of humor. One day, during my lecture on pain and acupuncture, Mr. X raised his hand and asked if I had ever heard of "alcoholic acupuncture." I indicated that I had not, and Mr X proceeded to tell me with a straight face that "alcoholic acupuncture is when you get stuck for the drinks." The class loved it. Most of his contributions in class, it should be noted, were of a more serious nature.

During the course of a single semester it was my pleasure to watch Mr. X change from a timid, withdrawn, unself-confident old person into a thoughtful, friendly, self-confident college student. I knew that Mr. X had conquered his self-doubts when he asked to take the final examination in the course. An audit student is not required to take examinations, as they do not receive formal course credit toward a degree. He chose to be evaluated along with the rest of the class, and he earned a respectable B on the final exam. Mr. X continues to take other courses at the University. This man's story is unique, and this is unfortunate. It should not be unique. Going back to college may not be the answer for all elderly people, but it should be noted that there is an answer for everyone somewhere. We must make the effort to find this answer.

A number of suggestions have been made for minimizing the sensory deterioration that can accompany the aging process. How do we best cope with that degree of sensory deficit that cannot be avoided? There are several answers to this question. The most extreme answer, the use of sensory aids, will be discussed in the next chapter. There are also some simple techniques that can be used to help us compensate for reduced sensory acuity. One important part of compensating is knowing what to compensate for. In general, the major categories of unavoidable sensory deficit in the elderly involve reduced visual acuity in dim light, color vision losses especially for the blue-violet end of the visible spectrum, and reduced hearing, especially for high frequency sounds. A deficit in near vision is also common in the aged, but this problem will be dealt with in the next chapter. None of these deficits presents a major obstacle to a person's normal everyday functioning. Adequate compensation may be achieved by using brighter light bulbs for reading, by exercising extra caution when driving at night or possibly giving up driving at night in extreme cases, and by not buying the "top of the line" in stereo equipment since the auditory system of an older person cannot appreciate the high frequency sound components.

The falling off in speech comprehension reported in the elderly can also be compensated for to some extent. If it is kept in mind that the deficit is greater in a noisy environment, one can train oneself to be more attentive to the speaker in such a situation. One can also learn to be more vigilant, just as a salesman can learn to remember customers' names. As vigilance is known to decrease in the elderly, they should make a conscious effort to increase their vigilance when conversing with others. Speech comprehension can also be improved by watching the speaker's lips, and by realizing that it is far better to ask someone to repeat something that was missed in a conversation than to get the wrong message.

There are some less obvious compensatory behaviors that might be mentioned in conjunction with decreased sensory capacities. The taste and smell modalities in the elderly have been reported to experience a decline. The older person should keep in mind that the senses of those around him or her may not be experiencing a similar decline. For instance, personal hygiene should not be neglected just because you cannot smell yourself. The entire pot of soup or bowl of salad should not be seasoned to your liking, because what is just right for you may be entirely too spicy for others. On the other hand, a younger person should try to be tolerant of an older person who slips up on points such as the above and attempt to educate them as tactfully as possible. The point here is that different people do in fact have different perceptual worlds. We should keep this in mind and make allowances for it when we come across someone who does not "see eye to eye" with us. There may be something other than stubbornness or stupidity causing a person to perceive the world other than we perceive it.

Chapter 12

MECHANICAL SENSORY AIDS

AS HAS been made quite clear in the preceding chapters, growing old involves a reduction in the acuity of our senses. We have the ability to minimize, but not completely avoid, these decreases in sensory acuity. In some people, the loss in sensitivity of our two most critical modalities, audition and vision, is so great that their ability to carry on normal daily activities is impaired. Such people would be well advised to inform themselves about the variety of mechanical aids that exist to assist a declining sensory system. The following pages present an overview of the topic of sensory aids.

Hearing Aids

The term "hearing aid" evokes in most of us a mental picture of a small, battery operated sound amplifying device that fits in the ear. Actually, hearing aids of various sorts existed for hundreds of years before the invention of the electrical model. The ear trumpet is one example of an early hearing aid; the speaking tube is another such example. These primitive hearing aids were quite helpful in cases of partial hearing loss: They served to channel sound waves directly into the auditory canal and to the eardrum, thereby amplifying the vibrations in that structure. The principle is the same (although much more effective) as cupping one's hand behind the ear to "catch" the sound waves. With the invention and improvement of the electrical hearing aid, ear trumpets and speaking tubes have been relegated to display cases in remote corners of medical museums.

Perhaps the most important development to date in the field of hearing aids occurred in the late 1940s, when transistorized components began to be used. This made possible both significant increases in reliability and significant decreases in size and weight of the devices. All electrical hearing aids contain a *microphone* to collect the sound waves and convert them into electrical impulses, an *amplifier* to increase the amplitude of the electrical impulses, and a *receiver* that converts the amplified electrical impulses into vibratory energy. There are two main types of receivers: the air-conduction receiver and the bone-conduction receiver. Air-conduction receivers are inserted into the ear canal and deliver sound vibrations to the eardrum. Bone-conduction receivers (sometimes called postauricular receivers) are worn behind the ear and stimulate the auditory system by delivering vibrations to the temporal bone. Air-conduction receivers are custom-made for each individual to insure a tight fit so that sound leakage out of the ear does not occur. Air-conductive and bone-conductive receivers are depicted in Figure 18. In general, air-conductive receivers are superior to bone-conductive receivers unless some special circumstance prevents an individual from wearing an insert-type receiver.

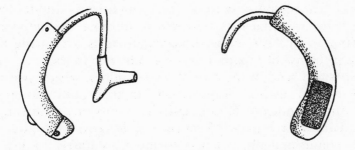

Figure 18. An insert-type air-conductive hearing aid, and a postauricular bone-conductive hearing aid.

An adequte hearing aid should transmit sound frequencies at least between the ranges of 400 Hz and 4000 Hz. As was noted in the chapter on hearing, few if any important speech sounds contain frequencies above 4000 Hz. Thus, there is little loss in speech intelligibility if a hearing aid does not transmit sound frequencies above this level. Similarly, it has been shown that there is no significant loss in speech intelligibility if a hearing aid does not transmit frequencies below 400 Hz.

Another important characteristic of adequate hearing aids is that they be designed to amplify high frequency sounds more than they do low frequency sounds. This differential amplification has two important purposes. First, presbycusis, the progressive hearing loss associated with aging, affects the higher frequencies. Second, you may recall from an earlier discussion that low frequency sounds displace a larger region of the basilar membrane than do higher sound frequencies. This means that low frequency sounds are more apt to mask high frequency sounds because, if a high and a low frequency sound are presented simultaneously, the area of the basilar membrane displaced by the low frequency sound could include the area displaced by the high frequency sound. By increasing the amplification of high frequency sounds, the modern hearing aid helps to resolve these potential problems.

Outside of cases of accidental injury or infection, most instances of hearing loss in the elderly involve both ears. In spite of this, the usual procedure (at least until recently) has been to wear a hearing aid only in one ear, whichever is slightly better. The belief was that it is sufficient to improve the individual's hearing in one ear. Now, however, there is a growing trend toward the use of binaural hearing aids (one in each ear). This is especially true in the case of deaf children, where specialists have noted a definite improvement in their ability to acquire and understand speech, especially in a noisy environment. Not surprisingly, a binaural hearing aid improves the ability of both young and old listeners to more accurately localize the source of a sound in space. This is because auditory localization depends upon binaural hearing cues, especially the relative loudness of the sound at the two ears. Binaural hearing aids can be of the type involving a single amplifier with a Y-lead going to each ear, or two separate amplifiers can be used, one for each ear. The single amplifier type is usually adequate if the degree of hearing loss is the same in each ear so that differential amplification is not necessary. Two separate amplifiers are preferred if the degree of sound amplification needed by each ear is not the same.

One category of hearing loss that has received little attention until recently is the case of the person with a hearing deficit in only one ear. There is a widespread belief that someone with good hearing in one ear should have little problem comprehending speech or responding normally to other sounds in the environment. However, hearing specialists are beginning to note a tendency among people with a unilateral (one-sided) hearing loss to report problems in conversing in a group situation or in places with background noise. Such people are at a disadvantage because their good ear must be used to pick up sounds and conversations that may originate on either side of the body. Sounds from the impaired side of the head are much less likely to be distinguished accurately, especially in the presence of extraneous noise. A hearing aid system has now been specifically designed for individuals with a unilateral hearing loss.

This system is referred to as *contralateral routing of signal,* or CROS. The CROS system consists of a microphone and amplifier to pick up sounds on the impaired side of the head, and a piece of tubing that transmits the sounds around the head to the unimpaired ear. The tubing can either be contained in the frame of eyeglasses or it can travel around the back of the head, concealed by the hair, to the good ear. The good ear is still able to respond to the sounds that it always heard, and in addition it can now be used to respond to amplified sounds that are transmitted from the opposite side of the head. Beneficial results with the CROS system have been noted in social situations (such as a cocktail party), occupational settings (such as a business meeting), educational situations (such as a classroom discussion), and family gatherings (such as a dinner table conversation) where speakers may be located on all sides of the hearing-impaired individual and where more than one person may be talking at the same time.

Electronic assistance is also available for the hard-of-hearing older person who may live alone, who has no real need to wear a hearing aid during the many hours spent without other people around. The major auditory needs that such a person might have would be to hear the telephone or the doorbell ring, and to listen to the radio or the television. As the greatest hearing loss in the elderly is in the high frequency range, it could benefit an older person living alone to have the telephone and the doorbell fitted with loud, low frequency, sound-generating devices. If the hearing loss is also pronounced in the low frequency range, a flashing light that is activated by the sound of the telephone or the doorbell can be used to alert the hearing-impaired person to answer the phone or the door.

A hearing impairment need not inhibit someone from listening to the radio or television. Rather than turning up the volume to levels that would disturb neighbors, it is possible to plug adapters into the set. The adapter leads the sound into an earpiece which the individual inserts into the ear canal, thereby permitting the hard-of-hearing person to enjoy programs without annoying other people in the vicinity.

An important factor in benefiting from any kind of hearing aid is the motivation of the affected individual to use. Some hard-of-hearing elderly people, because the onset of the hearing loss has been gradual and unnoticed by them, feel that they have no hearing problem, and that people around them are at fault for speaking indistinctly. It is sometimes extremely difficult to convince such a person of the value of a hearing aid. Other hearing-impaired older people are reluctant to use a hearing aid because they mistakenly believe that a hearing aid will speed the deterioration of their remaining hearing ability. This erroneous belief that a hearing aid can harm one's hearing is contributed to by the fact that hearing loss is usually progressive and continues to get worse even after an individual begins to use a hearing aid. Also, when a person using a hearing aid turns it off, the abrupt return to their deficient hearing level is so dramatic that by contrast it seems their hearing has become worse.

A person considering a hearing aid should first seek the advice of an audiologist to determine whether or not their particular kind of hearing loss can be helped by a hearing aid. Counseling can also be obtained to help the individual choose a hearing aid that will be most effective in dealing with his or her special circumstance. Some suppliers of hearing aids will permit a person to rent a hearing aid for a trial period ranging from a week to a month, in order to test its suitability, to discover the limitations of the aid, and to learn how to obtain maximum benefit from the device. This idea of a trial period is an excellent one and should be used by anyone considering the purchase of a hearing aid.

Recent advances in hearing aid technology have been so great that there are fewer and fewer instances of hearing impairment that cannot experience at least some level of improvement. What about the 300,000 or so persons in the United States who are profoundly deaf? These individuals derive no benefit from a hearing aid, and their chances of experiencing sound again (if they ever did) are usually rated as close to zero. The most typical finding in the profoundly deaf is that the auditory hair cells in the cochlea have been irreversibly damaged. Thus, no matter how greatly a hearing aid amplifies sound waves, no conversion of the sound waves into electrical nerve impulses can take place for the auditory nerve to transmit to the brain.

Although the auditory hair cells may be lacking, medical research has now shown that the auditory nerve retains at least partial function in many of the profoundly deaf. This means that if some method could be found for auditory stimulation to bypass the damaged or lacking auditory receptors and operate directly on the auditory nerve, some of the profoundly deaf might be able to experience sound.

In a series of fascinating experiments with deaf human volunteer subjects, it has been demonstrated that auditory sensations can be produced in such people by direct electrical stimulation of the auditory nerve through implanted electrode wires. Such stimulation bypasses the damaged hair cells and generates electrical impulses in the auditory nerve which then travel to the brain, where they are perceived as sound. To be sure, such artificial electrical stimulation has only resulted in the experiencing of simple buzzing or ringing sounds, but it demonstrates that the possibility exists for restoring some level of sound perception in many of the profoundly deaf.

Recently, researchers at the Stanford University Medical School's Department of Otolaryngology have been working on an electronic device that can be implanted in the cochlea of a deaf person. The device is sensitive to sound waves and contains electrodes which in turn electrically stimulate the auditory nerve. This cochlear implant is actually a substitute for the damaged auditory hair cells. While such a prosthesis is incapable of permitting the wearer to understand speech, profoundly deaf patients who have been surgically implanted with this device are able to perceive sounds such as the ring of a telephone or a door bell, and they have an additional cue to aid them in lip reading (they can now perceive the rhythm and cadence in the speaker's voice even though they cannot recognize different speech sounds). While further improvements in this kind of prosthetic device are likely, it is doubtful that in the forseeable future a cochlear implant will be developed that can exactly replicate the sound analyzing function ordinarily carried out by the many thousands of auditory hair cells in the cochlea.

The preceding pages point out that there are various steps that can be taken when an individual suffers a hearing impairment. Obviously, the preferred situation is to guard and protect one's hearing while it is intact so that these compensatory actions are unnecessary. In spite of the advances in hearing aid technology and in the area of cochlear implants, it is as yet impossible to artificially duplicate the remarkable capabilities of the human auditory system.

Visual Aids

Visual impairments can be due to an inability of the lens and cornea to focus light properly or to malfunctioning of the visual receptors on the retina. Many defects in the ability of the optical instruments of the eyeball (the lens and cornea) to focus light on the retina can be corrected with eyeglasses. The kind of corrective lens needed depends, of course, on the particular visual defect involved.

MYOPIA: In a small proportion of adults, a condition exists known as myopia. In this condition, the eyeball has changed its shape, becoming somewhat elongated. Because of this change in shape, light rays entering the eye are now brought to a focus in the vitreous fluid in front of the retina. The light rays then begin to diverge again, resulting in the formation of a blurred image on the retina. This condition is sometimes called "near-sightedness" in that all objects viewed at a distance from the affected individual will be blurred to some extent. The correction for myopia involves the use of concave eyeglass lenses for distant vision. The concave lenses will produce sufficient divergence in the light rays entering the eye that they will now be brought to an accurate focus on the retina. This kind of correction is diagrammed Figure 19.

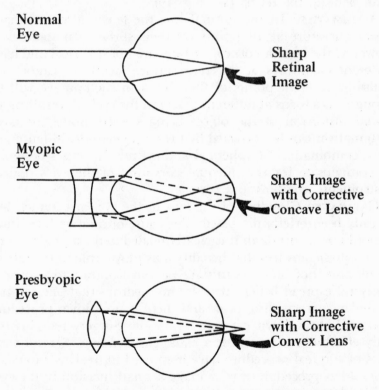

Figure 19. Examples of optical corrections for blurred vision.

PRESBYOPIA: A more common optical defect, especially found in people over the age of forty-five, is presbyopia. Here, the loss of eleasticity in the lens of the eye interferes with its ability to become short and thick when viewing an object close to the individual (accommodation). This progressive failure of accommodation causes the near point of distinct vision to recede farther and farther from the eye until near vision is seriously impaired. In the eye of the presbyopic individual, the image of near objects is brought to a focus behind the retina, resulting in a blurring of vision. The appropriate correction in this case is to use eyeglasses for near work, such as reading, that have convex lenses. Convex lenses produce the added convergence of light rays needed to bring near objects to a focus on, rather than behind, the retina (see Fig. 19).

ASTIGMATISM: In the normal eye, the lens and cornea have equal curvature at all points on their surface. In some eyes, however, the lens or corneal surfaces are not spherical and have different curvatures at different surface locations. Light rays entering different points of the cornea in such an eye will be brought to a focus at different places in the eyeball, resulting in visual distortion of the object being viewed. Some forms of astigmatism can be corrected by the use of cylindrical lenses, or by a combination of spherical and cylindrical lenses designed to compensate for the unequal curvature of the eye's optical instruments, the lens and cornea.

CATARACTS: Clouding of the lens of the eye, or cataract, has already been briefly discussed. The cause of cataract formation is not known, although it is clearly related to the aging process. Some physicians feel that heredity may play a role in the rate of development of cataracts in some people. Contrary to a surprisingly widespread belief, there are no eyedrops that one can use to make cataracts disappear, and there is no known procedure that will slow down cataract formation. Surgery remains the only effective treatment for a badly clouded lens. Several varieties of surgical procedure have been used in treating cataracts. The oldest procedure was to make a small incision in the eyeball and remove the entire lens with a special forceps, or with a small suction cup. A variety of this technique is to remove only the frontal layers of the lens, leaving the rear part of the lens capsule behind. More recently, a freezing method has been used, where an ice ball is formed in the cataract, which is attached to the tip of a probe. Then the clouded lens which is affixed to the tip of the probe can easily be removed through an incision in the eyeball. A newer technique in the treatment of cataracts involves the use of ultrasound waves to break up the clouded lens into small particles which can then be drained off by a suction pipette inserted into the eyeball.

After cataract surgery, the individual will need some way to compensate for the light focusing properties of the missing lens. One is not blind after cataract surgery, as some people mistakenly believe, but vision is blurred. Uncorrected vision after cataract surgery has been likened to viewing an object underwater. The standard choice of corrective procedures that used to face someone after cataract surgery was bifocals, which provide both reading and distance lenses at the same time, or two pairs of the eyeglasses, one for near vision and one for far vision. Most people found changing glasses to be a greater nuisance than learning to live with bifocals. More recently, a trend has developed for people who have had cataract surgery to wear contact lenses. These individuals will still need glasses for reading and other near work, because the contact lenses only benefit far vision. Another recent development in the treatment of cataracts is for the surgeon to remove the clouded lens in the usual fashion, but then to replace it with an artificial plastic lens. While this operation has a high rate of success, it is usually restricted to patients who cannot wear contact lenses for one reason or another. The implanted plastic lens does away with the need for bifocals or contact lenses, although patients who are fitted with the plastic lens still must wear reading glasses, as the plastic lens cannot change its shape (undergo accommodation) as the natural lens did.

BLINDNESS: It is clear that many defects in the ability of the lens and cornea to focus light onto the retina can be corrected with eyeglasses, contact lenses, or by surgery. What about the many thousands of individuals who are blind or near-blind because permanent damage has been done to the visual receptors on the retina? Until recently, the major sensory aids available to such people were a dog, a white cane, and a fairly small literature transcribed into braille; only a small percentage of the blind actually learn to use these limited aids. However, a number of recent technological advances in the area of sensory prosthesis have made it possible to significantly improve the lot of the blind and near-blind.

One recent development of importance for the blind is the so-called "laser cane," currently being used with success by a number of blind people as an aid in mobility. The cane sends out thin beams of light which strike and reflect back from obstacles in the path of the user, and warn him or her by generating auditory and tactile signals. With proper training a blind person can use the laser cane to detect street curbs, stair steps, moving objects, and even overhanging objects at head height (that a guide dog but not a human being could pass under) such as a police call box or a tree limb.

Also available at the present time is a battery operated, hand-held talking calculator Speech Plus®, which identifies in a clear voice each key as it is pressed. This invention permits a blind person to use a calculator without fear of pressing the wrong key and without having to ask a sighted person to read the answer aloud. Another recent invention for the blind is the Kurzweil Reading Machine®. This is a desk-top sized unit that can scan printed material and read sentences aloud in a clear (but metallic) voice at a rate of 150 words per minute. Although presently priced beyond the means of most people (around $50,000), it is expected that within a few years this reading machine will be available at a more reasonable price (about $5,000).

Another item now available is a "talking chess board" which, when a chess piece is moved, announces its color, name, and the coordinate square of the chess board. This device greatly simplifies chess playing for the blind. Of perhaps a more practical nature, a pocket-sized scanning instrument now exists which can identify and announce the denomination of paper money, thereby helping the blind avoid being victimized by unscrupulous people. Still another remarkable sensory aid for the blind is the Optacon® (which stands for Optical to Tactile Coversion). The Optacon permits blind people to read conventional printed material such as books, newspapers, and personal letters by converting the printing into tactile sensations which can be detected with the index finger. In one hand the user holds a small optical sensor about the size of a disposable cigarette lighter. The sensor is moved over the surface of the printed material, and the different printed letters are transduced into patterns of vibrations in a 1 by 1/2 inch array of tiny moving rods which can be felt with the index finger of the hand not holding the sensor. The vibrating rods are contained in a battery operated unit about the size and weight of a portable radio. With training, a blind person can use the Optacon to read at speeds up to 80 to 90 words per minute. This is well below the reading rate of sighted people, but well above the reading rates possible using conventional braille. Of course, the obvious advantage of the Optacon is that the blind individual is no longer limited to reading materials that have been transcribed into braille. In addition to opening up a new world of literature to the blind, the Optacon has proven to be invaluable for blind students pursuing their education and for blind people in occupations that were formerly restricted to sighted individuals. Work is currently underway to provide the Optacon with accessories that will permit it to talk, thereby making possible reading speeds up to 200 words per minute.

Another potentially beneficial sensory aid for the blind is the Tactile Vision Substitution System (TVSS). TVSS makes use of the touch receptors in the skin of the abdomen, permitting them to compensate after a fashion for the missing visual receptors on the retina. TVSS employs a miniature, battery-operated optical sensor worn in an eyeglass frame. Images are picked up by the sensor and converted into faint electrical impulses. These impulses are delivered by wires to an array of 1000 or more tiny surface electrodes attached to an elastic girdle which is worn over the stomach. The electrical impulses produce a vibratory sensation on the stomach when delivered to the electrodes. The shapes of different objects viewed by the optical sensor are reproduced as different patterns of vibrations on the abdominal skin of the TVSS user. In experimental tests, blind subjects have quickly learned to identify common objects such as a drinking glass or a telephone, and to walk around in a room full of furniture without bumping into anything. The TVSS system is still in the developmental stages, although it is clear from its succcess to date that it should be generally available within a few years.

The most exotic of the recent developments to aid the blind are those attempts at producing visual experiences by electrically stimulating the visual cortex of the brain through an array of implanted electrodes. The intent of this procedure is to bypass the damaged or absent visual receptors and to artificially activate brain regions that in sighted persons are excited when light strikes the retina. A television camera has been used as an optical sensor, with the output of the sensor being fed into a computer. The computer in turn controls patterns of electrical impulses that are delivered to electrode wires that have been implanted in the visual cortex of the subject. Using such a procedure, medical researchers have been successful in getting blind volunteer human subjects to "see" recognizable patterns and shapes. The two-dimensional patterns perceived by the subjects are crude and simple, being made up of flashes of light (called *phosphenes*) similar to the flashes of light we experience when we get poked in the eyeball or hit on the head. In one such experiment, a blind volunteer was able to recognize letters of the alphabet in the form of cortical stimulation-induced phosphenes at a rate of 30 letters per minute. This reading speed for "cortical braille" actually exceeded the subject's reading rate for conventional tactile braille.

While this kind of research is still in the experimental stage, scientists are hopeful that at some time in the future sufficient improvements will result in a useful aid for the blind. They are working toward a miniature system involving a small optical sensor that can be implanted in an eye socket. The sensor would scan the environment and transmit patterns of lightness and darkness to a miniature computer built into an eyeglass frame. The battery-powered computer would in turn convert the light patterns into electrical impulses which would be delivered directly to an array of electrodes permanently implanted in the visual cotex. Far from being an example of science fiction, such an outcome now appears feasible.

As the human life span becomes greater and greater, it follows that there will be an increasing number of people with varying degrees of sensory dysfunction in the population. It should be comforting that our understanding of the physiology of the sensory systems is such that in many cases we can keep sensory deficits to a minimum. The preceding pages have mentioned some of the ways partial sensory deficiencies can be dealt with; even in the extreme case of profound deafness or total blindness, there are compensatory measures that can be taken. Of course, there is at present no adequate substitute for the information-processing capacities of the human senses in their normal functioning state. However, the ingenuity and resourcefulness of the human intellect is such that technological advances of the kinds mentioned above are helping to reduce the feelings of utter dispair and depression that typically accompany severe sensory dysfunction.

INDEX